Great Playwrights

Other books in the
Profiles in History series:

Black Abolitionists
Black Women Activists
Hitler and His Henchmen
Leaders of the Civil Rights Movement
Pioneers of Human Rights
Rulers of Ancient Egypt
Terrorist Leaders

Great Playwrights

Profiles . in . History

Sandra Rabey Weisel, *Book Editor*

Bruce Glassman, *Vice President*
Bonnie Szumski, *Publisher*
Helen Cothran, *Managing Editor*

GREENHAVEN PRESS
An imprint of Thomson Gale, a part of The Thomson Corporation

THOMSON
✳
GALE

Detroit • New York • San Francisco • San Diego • New Haven, Conn.
Waterville, Maine • London • Munich

For more information, contact
Greenhaven Press
27500 Drake Rd.
Farmington Hills, MI 48331-3535
Or you can visit our Internet site at http://www.gale.com

LIBRARY OF CONGRESS CATALOGING-IN-PUBLICATION DATA

Great playwrights / Sandra Rabey Weisel, book editor.
p. cm. — (Profiles in history)
Includes bibliographical references and index.
ISBN 0-7377-2138-3 (lib. : alk. paper)
1. Drama—History and criticism. 2. Drama—Bio-bibliography. 3. Dramatists—Biography—Dictionaries. I. Weisel, Sandra Rabey. II. Series.
PN1623.G67 2005
809.2'003—dc22
[B]   2004045564

Contents

Chapter 1: Ancient Greeks Introduce Tragedy and Comedy

Chapter 2: The Legacy of the Elizabethans and Jacobeans

Chapter 3: Eastern Poets Stage Vivid Performances

Chapter 5: Americans Address the Human Condition

grief and guilt was a master of characterization and exposed the seedier sides of human behavior and sexuality in his dramas.

Foreword

Historians and other scholars have often argued about which forces are most influential in driving the engines of history. A favorite theory in past ages was that powerful supernatural forces—the gods and/or fate—were deciding factors in earthly events. Modern theories, by contrast, have tended to emphasize more natural and less mysterious factors. In the nineteenth century, for example, the great Scottish historian Thomas Carlyle stated, "No great man lives in vain. The history of the world is but the biography of great men." This was the kernel of what came to be known as the "great man" theory of history, the idea that from time to time an unusually gifted, influential man or woman emerges and pushes the course of civilization in a new direction. According to Carlyle:

> Universal History, the history of what man has accomplished in this world, is at bottom the History of the Great Men who have worked here. They were the leaders of men, these great ones; the modelers . . . of whatsoever the general mass of men contrived to do or to attain; all things that we see standing accomplished in the world are properly the outer material result. . . . The soul of the whole world's history, it may justly be considered, were the history of these [persons].

In this view, individuals such as Moses, Buddha, Augustus, Christ, Constantine, Elizabeth I, Thomas Jefferson, Frederick Douglass, Franklin Roosevelt, and Nelson

Mandela accomplished deeds or promoted ideas that sooner or later reshaped human societies in large portions of the globe.

The great man thesis, which was widely popular in the late 1800s and early 1900s, has since been eclipsed by other theories of history. Some scholars accept the "situational" theory. It holds that human leaders and innovators only react to social situations and movements that develop substantially on their own, through random interactions. In this view, Moses achieved fame less because of his unique personal qualities and more because he wisely dealt with the already existing situation of the Hebrews wandering in the desert in search of a new home.

More widely held, however, is a view that in a sense combines the great man and situational theories. Here, major historical periods and political, social, and cultural movements occur when a group of gifted, influential, and like-minded individuals respond to a situation or need over the course of time. In this scenario, Moses is seen as one of a group of prophets who over the course of centuries established important traditions of monotheism; and over time a handful of ambitious, talented pharaohs led ancient Egypt from its emergence as the world's first nation to its great age of conquest and empire. Likewise, the Greek playwrights Sophocles and Euripides, the Elizabethan playwright Shakespeare, and the American playwright Eugene O'Neill all advanced the art of drama, leading it to its present form.

The books in the Profiles in History series chronicle and examine in detail the leading figures in some of history's most important historical periods and movements. Some, like those covering Egypt's leading pharaohs and the most influential U.S. presidents, deal with national leaders guiding a great people through good times and bad. Other volumes in the series examine the leaders of important, constructive social movements, such as those that sought to abolish slavery in the nineteenth century and fought for human rights in the twentieth century. And some, such as the one on Hitler and his henchmen, profile far less constructive, though no less historically important, groups of leaders.

Each book in the series begins with a detailed essay providing crucial background information on the historical period or movement being covered. The main body of the volume consists of a series of shorter essays, each covering an important individual in that period or movement. Where appropriate, two or more essays are devoted to a particularly influential person. Some of the essays provide biographical information; while others, including primary sources by or about the person, focus in on his or her specific deeds, ideas, speeches, or followers. More primary source documents, providing further detail, appear in an appendix, followed by a thorough, up-to-date bibliography that guides interested readers to further research. Overall, the volumes of the Profiles in History series offer a balanced view of the march of civilization by demonstrating how certain individuals make history and at the same time are products of the deeds and movements of their predecessors.

Introduction

From curtain up to curtain down, an audience sees more, hears more, and learns more of the characters on-stage and their predicaments than of real people audience members may have known for years. Playwrights, although constrained by the limitations of time and the stage, must somehow craft dramas that engage and entertain, tell believable stories, build and resolve conflict, and bring characters to life. In this sense playwrights are the true inventors of virtual reality. The tools of their artifice are not 3-D graphics and sound effects but the dramatic conventions of plot, character, and dialogue.

With the use of precise plotting, exposition, and condensation, playwrights can quickly pull audiences into the tangles of their tales. They build suspense through strategic timing, carefully controlling the revelation of critical information. They replace the routine and mundane with conflict, and they purposefully order scenes to engage their characters in dramatic moments.

Playwrights must infuse their characters with real human emotions and foibles and then allow audiences insights into the characters' personalities and motivations. Audiences are often privy to a character's innermost thoughts—spoken onstage—and often know more about the characters than the characters know about one another. This omniscient perspective intensifies the viewer's empathy and reactions, and helps remove the barrier between audience and action.

For the sake of clarity and communication, playwrights must also endow their characters with an articulateness that exceeds the norm. "A dramatist has to write eloquently, which is to say that he has to achieve a level of speech, not for a character but for whole plays, that is far higher than our talk in life," writes Eric Bentley, author of *The Life of the Drama*. This can be achieved in many styles—poetic verse, prose, dialect— as well as by altering the cadences and content of ordinary speech.

Three classic dramas by great playwrights from different countries and eras demonstrate the ability of a dramatist to convey reality through artifice.

Romeo and Juliet

In William Shakespeare's romantic tragedy *Romeo and Juliet*, written in the mid-1590s, two young people pass from childhood into adulthood as they fall deeply in love. Shakespeare compresses the action of the play— the lovers' meeting, courtship, secret marriage, and demise—into four frantic days. Conflict stems from the hero's and heroine's families who are enemies. Their bitterness and hatred are in stark opposition to the pure love between their young offspring, Romeo and Juliet.

Shakespeare deftly plots the paths of the lovers with tragic timing: Juliet drinks a sleeping potion to feign death to avoid marrying another; Romeo thinks Juliet is dead because he never receives the Friar's message explaining the deception; the grief-stricken Romeo drinks a deadly poison beside her body in the vault; Juliet awakens to a lifeless Romeo and kills herself with his dagger rather than live without him.

The play is distinguished as much by Shakespeare's extraordinary use of language as by its tragic plot. Romeo and Juliet speak in iambic pentameter (poetry composed of rhyming lines of five pairs of syllables, with stress on the second syllable of each pair) and blank verse (iambic meter written without rhyme). These poetic forms enhance the play's message; Shakespeare accents and rhymes important words and ideas to reinforce his themes and focus viewers' attention.

A Doll's House

The success of Norwegian playwright Henrik Ibsen's *A Doll's House*, written in 1879, depends on giving an element of classical tragedy—the flawed protagonist, suffering the consequences of past actions—a fresh interpretation, with a modern setting and a heroine who not only does not die, but literally slams the door on her old life to begin a new one.

Some critics charge that Ibsen's play is in a way unrealistic: On the surface, *A Doll's House* is a domestic drama with elements of melodrama—unlikely coincidences, threats, and secrets—that stretch the audience's credulity. Its main characters, for example, all have tangled relationships and histories. Nora Helmer is the sheltered, frivolous wife of domineering, dismissive banker Torvald Helmer. In a desperate move to help Torvald recover from past illness, Nora forged loan papers to borrow money from bank barrister Krogstad, whom she has not yet repaid. Outwardly gay, Nora is inwardly guilty and tormented. Krogstad threatens to reveal Nora's deception to her husband if Torvald replaces him at the bank with Nora's friend Kristina, who was once romantically involved with Krogstad. When Kristina and Krogstad rekindle their love, however, Krogstad is moved to cancel the debt, and even though Torvald learns the truth, the Helmer household, it seems, might be restored to normal. But the resolution is not that simple.

The startling realism of *A Doll's House* lies not in the plot, but in the complex personalities of the characters and their relationships to one another, and in the way

Nora Helmer, in particular, changes. Ibsen's play is an unflattering reflection of the society of his day, in which women really were powerless, submissive, near-property, confined to domestic roles, judged worthy only inasmuch as they served and pleased their husbands. Torvald viciously turns on Nora when her forgery and their indebtedness is revealed. Instead of appreciating her resourcefulness, or selfless motives, or inner strength when he was ill, he demeans her as a liar and a stupid woman and blames her for ruining his reputation and his life (because, Ibsen implies, Torvald's life *is* his reputation). Then, with the face-saving forgiveness of the debt, Torvald reverts to his comfortable position as master of the household, and of Nora, his pet.

Ibsen has made Nora too multifaceted to put her meekly back in her doll's house, however. The audience knows now that although she indeed has frivolous traits, Torvald underestimates her. Though her final exit from home and family was a shocking act in Ibsen's day, audiences ever since have empathized with Nora's transformation into an empowered, independent person.

The simple, straightforward dialogue in *A Doll's House* reinforces the play's realism. As Ibsen biographer Michael Meyer writes in *Henrik Ibsen, Plays: Two*, "[Ibsen] achieved the most powerful and moving effect by the highly untraditional methods of extreme simplicity and economy of language."

Death of a Salesman

In his drama *Death of a Salesman*, awarded the 1949 Pulitzer Prize, Arthur Miller portrays the downfall of traveling salesman Willy Loman by skillfully intertwining scenes in the present with scenes that reenact Willy's memories of better times and that expose the illusions he clings to desperately. This juxtaposition of scenes reflects Willy's loosening grip on reality as he struggles with the crises in his life. For instance, Willy's loss of employment and the failure of his son Biff are played against Willy's inflated memories of his success as a salesman and Biff's glory days as a high school football star.

Miller sets his flawed hero on a downward spiral toward suicide by burdening him with circumstances that kill his dreams and destroy his self-esteem. But to maintain believability and audience sympathy for the downtrodden salesman, Miller puts Willy in situations that remind audiences of themselves or people they know: Willy is guilty of an affair; he is fired from his job as he nears retirement age; and he has a contentious relationship with his eldest son.

The audience gains a deeper understanding of Willy's decline by witnessing the behavior of other characters toward him. His wife is overprotective; Biff is at first disrespectful and later brutally honest; and son Happy is in denial about his father's faltering state of mind. Willy's boss addresses the salesman's loss of effectiveness by firing him, and Willy's neighbor exposes the out-of-work salesman's false pride when Willy refuses to accept a job with him. The audience learns even more of Willy's mental deterioration by eavesdropping on his mumblings to his brother and others who are not really there.

Miller also draws the audience into the world onstage with the natural, lifelike quality of his characters' language. The characters' speech is full of common expressions and clichés—a dime a dozen, life is short, a man of few words, laying it on the line, on the right track, and it comes with the territory. Miller's gift is in making such commonplace expressions, and the famous phrase, "Attention must be paid," eloquent.

Great Playwrights

Shakespeare, Ibsen, and Miller are three of the greatest among the many since the days of the ancient Greeks who have succeeded in writing dramas that speak to modern audiences and promise to endure. In the pages that follow are the real-life stories of these and other great playwrights from around the world and across the centuries who have mastered the art of artificial reality, creating moving and memorable imitations of life for the stage.

Profiles · in · History

Ancient Greeks Introduce Tragedy and Comedy

Aeschylus: The Father of Tragedy

Richmond Lattimore

Although tragedies had been performed in Athens prior to the works of Aeschylus (ca. 513–ca. 455 B.C.), his plays have made him the father of tragedy for a couple of reasons. First, his plays are the earliest surviving tragedies from the ancient world; secondly, they reflect his significant contributions to the development of this dramatic form. His seven surviving plays, including *The Persians, The Seven Against Thebes*, and the trilogy *Oresteia*, show an evolution in the use of various performing conventions—the chorus, dialogue between actors, dancing, and costuming. His creativity was rewarded with first prize more than a dozen times at the Great Dionysia, the annual dramatic competition in Athens.

In this excerpt from the introduction to *The Complete Greek Tragedies: Aeschylus*, Richmond Lattimore provides a glimpse into the playwright's life, the Greek world as he knew it, and the form that tragedy took. Lattimore was considered a leading translator of Greek classical literature. He, along with Greek translator and University of Chicago classics instructor David Grene, edited numerous books on the Greek tragedies of Aeschylus, Euripides, and Sophocles. Lattimore was professor emeritus at Bryn Mawr College in Pennsylvania at the time of his death in 1984.

Richmond Lattimore, "Introduction to the *Oresteia*," *The Complete Greek Tragedies, Volume 1, Aeschylus,* edited by David Grene and Richmond Lattimore. Chicago: University of Chicago Press, 1959. Copyright © 1959 by the University of Chicago. Reproduced by permission.

❧   ❧   ❧

Aeschylus, the son of Euphorion, was born in the last quarter of the sixth century B.C., probably about 513 or 512 B.C. The great Persian Wars occurred during his early manhood, and he fought, certainly at Marathon (where his brother was killed in action) and probably also at Artemisium, Salamis, and Plataea. He is said to have begun at an early age to write tragedies; his first victory [at the Great Dionysia] was in 484 B.C. In or about 476 B.C. he visited Sicily and, at the instance of Hieron [I, tyrant] of Syracuse, [the great lyric poet] Pindar's friend, produced *The Women of Etna* at the new city of Etna which Hieron had founded. In 472 he produced his *Persians* at Athens, with [the Athenian statesman and general] Pericles as his choregus (or official sponsor) and re-produced it, presumably in the next year, in Sicily. Back in Athens in 468, he was defeated by the young Sophocles, but won again in 467 with a set of plays including *The Seven Against Thebes*. In 458 he presented the *Oresteia* (*Agamemnon*, *The Libation Bearers*, *The Eumenides*). He died in Gela, Sicily, in 456 or 455 B.C., leaving behind him an epitaph which might be rendered as follows:

> Under this monument lies Aeschylus the Athenian, Euphorion's son, who died in the wheatlands of Gela. The grove of Marathon with its glories can speak of his valor in battle. The long-haired Persian remembers and can speak of it too.

He left behind more than seventy plays (the exact number is uncertain), of which seven have survived. They are *The Suppliants*, *The Persians*, *The Seven Against Thebes*, *Prometheus Bound*, *Agamemnon*, *The Libation Bearers*, *The Eumenides*. He is said to have won first prize thirteen times while he lived, but after his death his tragedies were often produced again, and in competition with living poets he won more prizes still.

An Uncertain Birth Date

It would be interesting to know how old Aeschylus was when he wrote his known and dated plays. But the date of his birth is quite uncertain, though the year 525/4 is commonly given as if it were an established fact. It is true enough that apparently independent authorities give ages at the time of Marathon and at time of death which agree with this scheme. However, the birth date may very easily be accounted for by the rule-of-thumb method, favored by Greek chronologists, of taking an important event in a man's life and counting back forty years to an estimated date of birth. Thus the traditional birth date of Thucydides [author of the *History of the Peloponnesian War*] is 471 (from the outbreak of the war he recorded in 431); of Aristophanes, 445 (from the production of his masterpiece, *The Frogs*, in 405). Both these dates are bad (there are many parallels), and the one for Aeschylus is no more convincing. An age of forty at his first victory is suspect, not only because it tallies so neatly with a known method of reckoning, but because it is in itself unlikely that a man who utterly eclipsed his rivals in subsequent reputation, so that they are now very little more than bare names, should have had to wait so long before scoring his first success. A less popular but more attractive tradition would make him born in 513 or 512, but here also we may be dealing with estimates based on known and dated events, such as battles and dramatic productions.

Ancient authorities also tell us a few other things about Aeschylus which would be interesting if we could believe them. It is said that he left Athens for Sicily in chagrin because he was defeated by Simonides, the great lyric poet, in a competition for writing the epitaph of the dead at Marathon, or because he was defeated by Sophocles in dramatic competition, or because he disliked Athenian politics. The defeats are real, but they do not tally, chronologically, with the visits to Sicily; on the contrary, after losing to Sophocles, Aeschylus stayed in Athens and won first prize with *The Seven Against Thebes* and its related dramas the next year, which is quite different from going off to Sicily in a huff. If one may guess at why he went to Sicily, it was because Sicily was the America of that day, the new Greek world, rich, generous, and young, with its own artists but without the tradition of perfected culture which Old Greece had built up. . . . We do not know much about the personal character of Aeschylus and can make little critical use of what we do know. The epitaph shows he was proud of his military record, but this scarcely helps us to understand *The Persians*, *The Seven Against Thebes*, or *Agamemnon*. We must approach Aeschylus, not from the biographies, but from his own plays.

Early Tragedy

From the time of the almost legendary Thespis,[1] a full generation before the earliest tragedy we possess, dramatic performances of some sort had been regularly produced at Athens. In origin, they must have been a special local development of the choral lyric—sacred, occasional, provincial, public—which was alive in all the cities of Greece. But the early phases of the course by which dramatic lyric was transformed into lyric drama are now invisible to us. We can recognize certain ingredients, or essential features. Early drama was choral, and the life of Attic[2] tragedy shows the indispensable chorus

1. considered the originator of Greek tragedy and the first winner of the Great Dionysia in ca. 534 B.C.   2. Attica was a region of ancient Greece around Athens.

to the end, though the actors steadily invade the preserves of the chorus until, at the close of the fifth century, Euripides is using it sometimes in a most perfunctory manner, as if it were a convention he could not get rid of but might otherwise have preferred to do without. Early drama was sacred, having to do with the cult of divinities, and particularly with the cult of Dionysus: on the formal side, it was performed to the end on ground devoted to that god and before his priest; but developed tragedy did not have to be *about* Dionysus, and seldom was. Like most choral lyric, it was given through the medium of a formal competition. The early tragic poets drew, for narrative material and for metrical forms, on an already rich and highly developed tradition of non-dramatic poetry, epic and lyric. They also drew, no doubt, on the unwritten and almost inarticulate experience of a living people, on folk memory and folklore, cult and ritual and ceremony and passion play and mystery play. But tragedy did not grow out of such elements. It was made. Concerning the makers, we know little indeed about Thespis, Pratinas, Choerilus, Phrynichus. Tragedy, for us, begins with Aeschylus.

By or during the career of Aeschylus, the features of Greek tragedy become fixed. At an Athenian festival, three player-groups, each consisting of two (later three) actors and chorus, act out competitively four-drama sets. The material is based on stories told or indicated in previous Greek legend. Tragedy is heroic. The costumes are formal, physical action restrained and without violence; naturalism is neither achieved nor desired. Aeschylus himself, and his older contemporary Phrynichus before him, experimented with dramatic stories taken from contemporary history, and of these we have *The Persians*, dealing with the repulse of Xerxes [king of Persia from 486 to 465 B.C.] and his forces. This was a success, but circumstances in this case were favorable to special occasional drama, for the defeat of Persia was the proudest achievement of Greek history. And, even here, the play is *about* the Persians, not the Greeks, the setting is Persia, and only Persian individuals are named. Remoteness from the immediate here-and-now, required by tragedy and guaranteed by legendary material, is here to a great extent achieved by placing the scene in the heart of Persia, so far away and guarded from Greeks that to the audience it might have seemed almost as legendary as the Troy of Hector or the Thebes of Oedipus. A drama dealing directly with [Athenian statesmen] Themistocles and Pericles or with the war between Athens and Aegina would have been neither desired by the poet nor tolerated by his audience.

Dramas Based on Epic Poems

The body of legend on which Aeschylus and the other tragic poets drew was composed of the epic poems of Homer and his successors and constituted a loose and informal, but fairly comprehensive, history of the world as the Greeks knew it. Typical sources in this complex were the *Iliad* and the *Odyssey;* the "Epic Cycle," or series of subsequent epics which filled out the story of Troy and dealt in detail with its occasions and aftereffects; the epics that told the story of Thebes; and numerous other narratives either written down or transmitted through unwritten oral tradition. The dramatist rarely worked directly from the main body of the *Iliad* or the *Odyssey;* the less authoritative minor texts were more popular. The dramatist seems not to have felt free to invent his material outright, but he could—in fact, he must—choose among variants, expand or deepen and interpret character, generally shape the story on the trend of his own imagination.

Sophocles: Winner of Dramatic Competitions

Thomas J. Sienkewicz

Sophocles (ca. 496–406 B.C.) was one of the most victorious, if not the most triumphant, of the ancient Greek playwrights who competed in the dramatic competition called the Great Dionysia. More than ninety of his plays were among his first-place wins, and he never placed lower than second. He defeated such accomplished dramatists as the elder Aeschylus and the younger Euripides. Sophocles was an imitator of the epic poet Homer and a master of character development, dialogue, and the use of the chorus. Among his surviving plays are *Antigone*, *Oedipus Rex*, and *Oedipus at Colonus*. Besides being a playwright, Sophocles was a patriot—a great lover of Athens. He held public office and served as a general with Pericles in the Revolt of Samos, a conflict that forced democracy on the Greek island.

In the following piece about Sophocles, excerpted from the *Critical Survey of Drama: Foreign Language Series*, Thomas J. Sienkewicz chronicles the life of the ancient Greek playwright, including his education, work, patriotism, and disputed piety. Sienkewicz teaches in the classics department at Monmouth College in Monmouth, Illinois.

Thomas J. Sienkewicz, *Critical Survey of Drama: Foreign Language Series*, edited by Frank N. Magill. Englewood Cliffs, NJ: Salem Press, 1986. Copyright © 1986 by Frank N. Magill. All rights reserved. Reproduced by permission.

The main events of Sophocles' life are known from several ancient sources, including inscriptions and especially an Alexandrian biography which survives in the manuscript tradition. While it is difficult at times to distinguish fact from anecdote in these sources, even the fiction is a useful gauge of Sophocles' image and reputation in antiquity.

Sophocles' lifetime coincides with the glorious rise of Athenian democracy and Athens' naval empire and with the horrors of the Peloponnesian War. Born a generation later than Aeschylus and a generation earlier than Euripides, Sophocles won dramatic victories over both of these playwrights. He was born c. 496 B.C. to Sophilus, a wealthy industrialist and slave owner from the Athenian *deme* [district] of Colonus. While Sophocles generally avoids personal references in his plays, his love for his native Colonus is evident in his last work, *Oedipus at Colonus*, and especially in the famous Colonus ode of that play.

Sophocles received a good education. According to ancient sources, as a youth he won competitions in wrestling and in music. His music teacher, Lamprus, was known for his epic and conservative compositions, for which he was ranked in his day with the great lyric poet Pindar. Sophocles himself is said to have been chosen to lead the victory song with lyre after the Athenian sea victory at Salamis in 480 B.C.

Lover of Athens

The patriotism of Sophocles was well-known in antiquity. In the ancient biography, he is called *philathenaiotatos*, "a very great lover of Athens," and, unlike both

Aeschylus and Euripides, he is said never to have left his native city for the court of a foreign king. Sophocles was also unlike his fellow dramatists in that he held public office several times: In 443/442, he was *Helleno-tamias*, a financial overseer of the Delian League in Athens; in 441/440, he was general along with Pericles in the Samian Revolt. Sophocles may have been general again, around 427, this time with Nicias; and in 413, he was elected *proboulos*, a member of a special executive committee. . . . No clear conclusions concerning the dramatist's political sentiments can be derived from Sophocles' political career, especially since fifth century Athenian democracy often survived on noncareer appointments from among its citizens. . . . Evidence shows that Sophocles was not politically detached, but rather, very much involved in the political and intellectual life of his day. The ancient biography mentions that Sophocles established a *thiasos*, or religious guild, in honor of the Muses. Other members of this intellectual group are unknown, but it may have included Sophocles' good friend, the historian Herodotus, whom the dramatist occasionally used as a source and to whom he wrote an ode.

Record Number of Victories

Sophocles won his first dramatic victory in 468 B.C. by defeating Aeschylus, probably with a group which included a *Triptolemus*, now lost. Whether this was Sophocles' first dramatic competition is not known, but it is recorded that the playwright went on to win twenty-three more victories, to earn second place many times, and third place never. With four plays in each production, this means that ninety-two out of Sophocles' approximately 124 dramas won for him first prizes. This great contemporary success contrasts strikingly with the career of Euripides, who won first place only five times.

Sophocles did not compete in 467 B.C. but probably won second place to Aeschylus' Danaid trilogy in 463(?) B.C.

Unfortunately, no plays from Sophocles' earliest years survive. The earliest extant play is probably *Ajax*, from the early 440's B.C. In his *Moralia*, Plutarch distinguishes three periods of Sophoclean style: a "weighty" period with Aeschylean similarities; a "harsh and artificial stage"; and a final group "most suited to express character and best." No extant plays, except perhaps *Ajax*, belong to the first two periods. Since the categories themselves, with their progression toward increasing worth, are obviously peripatetic [of Aristotelian philosophy] in origin, it is doubtful that these periods can be accepted as reliable statements about Sophoclean drama.

In 441 B.C., Sophocles probably produced *Antigone*, for which he may have won first prize, since the *hypothesis*, or ancient introduction, to this play states that the dramatist was elected general in 441/440, based upon the merit of *Antigone*. The Athenian democracy of that period was perfectly capable of making political appointments on such an apolitical basis. Other ancient sources imply that Sophocles saw no military action as general in the Samian Revolt that year but that he did travel to Ionia with the Athenian fleet.

Sophocles was certainly back in Athens in 438, when he won first prize with unknown plays against an Euripidean group which included *Alcestis*. The dating of *The Women of Trachis* is perhaps the most fiercely debated of all extant Sophoclean tragedies, but the stylistic and thematic similarities of this play to the firmly dated *Alcestis* make possible at least an approximate dating of *The Women of Trachis* to the period between 435 and 429.

In 431, Sophocles, competing with an unknown group of plays, came in second to the dramatist Euphorion, Aeschylus' son. Euripides came in third in that year with *Mēdeia* (431 B.C.; *Medea*). Sophocles made no production at the Greater Dionysia of 428. *Electra* is another play which is difficult to date accurately, but, based upon its links with Euripides' *Ēlektra* (413 B.C.; *Electra*), Sophocles' play can at least be dated to the decade beginning 420 B.C., except for the year 415, when it is known that Sophocles made no production. Only the last two extant plays are firmly dated: *Philoctetes*, which won for him first prize in 409 B.C., and *Oedipus at Colonus*, produced posthumously in 401 B.C. by Sophocles' grandson of the same name, which also won for him first prize.

The Cult of Asclepius

In addition to his patriotism, Sophocles was also noted for his piety. Specifically, he is linked with the cult of the healing god Asclepius, whose cult the dramatist helped establish in Athens in 420 B.C. Sophocles' paean to Asclepius was quite famous in antiquity and still survives in fragments. Sophocles was a priest of the hero Halon, who was ritually connected with Asclepius and under whose epithet, Dexion or "Receiver," Sophocles was honored posthumously. Such associations with public cults, however, were distinct in fifth century [B.C.] Athens from intellectual belief, and the classical view of Sophocles as calm, pious, and moderate has come to be questioned by such modern scholars as C.H. Whitman, who notes that the extant tragedies exhibit little of that blind piety which tradition links with the dramatist. Sophocles' true religious sentiments are lost behind the poetic veil of his tragedies.

There are indications in ancient sources that Sophocles had a troubled family life in his old age. The playwright had two sons: Iophon by Nicostrata and Ariston by the Sicyonian woman Theoris. Iophon was a dramatist in his own right and even competed against his father at least once. Less is known about Ariston, except that his son, Sophocles, was so favored by the grandfather that Iophon brought a lawsuit to have the old man made a legal ward of his son on the grounds of senility. Sophocles, speaking in his own defence at the trial, is said to have stated: "If I am Sophocles, I am not insane; if I am insane, I am not Sophocles." When Sophocles concluded by reciting lines from *Oedipus at Colonus*, his work in progress, the case was dismissed.

In March of 406, at the *proagon*, or preview to the Greater Dionysia, Sophocles dressed a chorus in mourning for the recent death of Euripides. This appearance at the *proagon* is evidence for a Sophoclean production in that year, but Sophocles must have died shortly after the dramatic festival, because in Aristophanes' *The Frogs*, produced in early 405, Sophocles is mentioned as already dead. Despite Sophocles' advanced age, the ancient sources still sought to embellish his death with several spurious causes: that he choked on a grape (like Anacreon), that he became overexerted while reciting *Antigone*, or that he died for joy after a dramatic victory. More reliable is the report that Sophocles' family was granted special permission from the Spartan general Lysander to bury the dramatist in his family plot on the road to Decelea, where the Spartans maintained a garrison. Death thus spared Sophocles from witnessing the complete collapse of the Athenian empire and the submission of Athens to Sparta in 405 to 404 B.C.

Aristophanes: Comedic Poet with a Bawdy Bent

Eugene O'Neill Jr.

Aristophanes' (ca. 445–ca. 388 B.C.) comedies are the only such works that have survived the centuries. He was born in a time when Athens was at war, and it is against this backdrop that most of his stories are set. Not unlike the comics of today, Aristophanes employed the use of dirty jokes, profanities, and obscenities to make his audiences laugh. He was also relentless in his ridicule of others, especially of the tragic poet Euripides, and he was a master at portraying oppositional forces—the rich and the poor, the young and the old, the powerful and the oppressed.

In his introduction to *The Complete Greek Drama*, Eugene O'Neill Jr. describes Aristophanes' approach to comedic drama and argues that the playwright had two sides to his character: a sharp-edged wit and a sensitive side. O'Neill, the eldest son of American dramatist Eugene O'Neill, was an assistant professor of the Greek classics and English at Yale University. He also taught at Princeton University and other colleges, published articles and reviews on Greek drama, and worked as a radio announcer. He died in 1950.

Eugene O'Neill Jr., "General Introduction," *The Complete Greek Drama: All the Extant Tragedies of Aeschylus, Sophocles, and Euripides, and the Comedies of Aristophanes and Menander, in a Variety of Translations, Volume 1,* edited by Whitney J. Oates and Eugene O'Neill Jr. New York: Random House, 1938.

🐝 🐝 🐝

Son of Philippus and Zenodora, [Aristophanes] was born about 445 B.C. in the Cydathenaean deme [district] in Attica. Typical of such information as we do possess about the poet are the facts that his family owned land in Aegina [an island off the southeast coast of Greece], and that he was bald at an early age. He aroused the ire but successfully weathered the attacks of the demagogue Cleon. He began to write when he was very young, and his first play, *The Banqueters*, was produced in 427 B.C., when he was but eighteen. He composed about forty comedies in all, but we do not know how often he was victorious [at the Great Dionysia]. On several occasions he brought out his plays under other names, but we do not know why he did this. The date of his death is uncertain, but it must have been later than 387. The ancient critics, who could compare his merits with those of his contemporaries, unanimously regarded him as the greatest of the poets of the Old Comedy. The result of this is that only Aristophanes has come down to us, and we have to base our judgments of the Old Comedy solely on the work of its most eminent artist. We must remember that we may not be dealing with what is typical of the comic drama of the time, but rather with something exceptional and revolutionary, advanced beyond its time.

Representative or not, for us it is unique. There has never been anything quite like it since, and regrettably there will never be anything quite like it again. The effect of the initial impact of these plays is one of bewilderment. One rubs one's eyes and wonders whether it really can have happened. A closer acquaintance and a bit of sober reflection disclose a number of distinct reasons for astonishment. The first of these is the absolute freedom of speech which the comic poet of the fifth century enjoyed. He might make fun, banteringly or bitterly, thoroughly and repeatedly, of anything; no person, no institution, no god, enjoyed the slightest vestige of immunity, and the Athenian populace seems to have enjoyed these libels and slanders so hugely that they did not even require that they be always amusing.

Loaded with Obscenities

Equally astonishing is the pervading obscenity of the Old Comedy. This is so abundant and so varied that it cannot be ignored or excised. It is so closely interwoven into almost every part of these plays that to expurgate is to destroy. A bowdlerized Aristophanes may offer a selection of passages well adapted to teach Attic Greek to schoolboys, but it is not Aristophanes. It may even illustrate certain aspects of Attic life and it will contain some incomplete passages of fine lyric poetry, but what has been taken away is the very part of his work which the poet clearly took the greatest delight in composing. On the other hand the misguided hypocrite who salves his conscience and saves his face by misrepresenting Aristophanes' bawdiness as something too healthy to be prurient does the poet a disservice more subtle and more harmful than the honest and busy expurgator. There is no escaping the fact that Aristophanes wrote just as obscenely as he could on every possible occasion. If we would appreciate him properly we should bear this in mind and endeavour to cultivate the same attitude that he had; the most unhealthy approach is the denial of the obvious in the name of healthiness.

Another feature of these comedies that immediately strikes us is the lordly ease with which their author has evidently composed them. This is inseparably connected with another equally remarkable feature of them, their dramaturgical ineptitude. Almost all of them are very badly constructed. They have nothing approaching unity; their plots are never worked out in any satisfactory fashion, and they abound in the most incredible inconsistencies. Yet they are obviously written by a man of magnificent gifts whom we cannot reasonably suppose to have been incapable of removing such blemishes; indeed, his latest comedies show indubitably that he could turn out as well integrated a play as anyone could desire. In his earlier work, on the other hand, it is clear that he just did not care about such things, and this observation gives us the clue to the proper appreciation of his work.

Brilliance and Wit

The distinguishing characteristic of Aristophanes is his brilliant insouciance. Endowed by nature with an intellect of an exceptionally high order and an imagination inexhaustibly fertile, he exercised his talents in a medium ideally suited to them. His best comedies are nothing but concatenations of splendid and dazzling conceits which follow one another in breathless abundance. He is never at a loss [as to] what to invent next; indeed, he hardly ever has time fully to exploit the humorous possibilities of one motif before he is occupied with another. A mind of this sort has no use for consistency, and that stodgy virtue may best be cultivated by the lesser talents, who need all the virtues they can get. An Aristophanes should not degrade himself by pretending to be an ordinary mortal.

It is from this point of view that we must approach him if we would avoid misunderstanding him. His brilliant insouciance makes him a lovable rogue, and we must not forget that Plato adored him. He has naturally been misunderstood, grossly and variously. He has a lot to say about himself, but hardly a word of it can be taken seriously. This would be an easy deduction from the quality of his mind, but he repeatedly proves it by his actions, for he blandly denies doing what he plainly and frequently does. His views on political and social questions have been eagerly and ponderously analysed, but this is mostly a waste of time and energy. He hated Cleon, so much is clear, but when he came to put his hate into a comedy it stifled his wit, and the result was *The Knights*, one of his poorest plays. It is safe to say that whenever his wit is functioning properly we have no hope of discovering what his real feelings were. . . .

His Softer Side

Brilliance . . . was not his only gift, and his heart was as sensitive as his mind was keen. The soft side of his personality expresses itself in his lyrics, and here he astounds and delights us, at one moment with idyllic songs of the countryside, at another with lines of infinite tenderness and sympathy, particularly towards old men. Often in the midst of a lyric passage of great warmth and beauty something will touch off his wit, and a sentence that has begun in a gentle and sympathetic spirit will end with a devastating personal jibe or an uproarious bit of obscenity. The two sides of the poet's nature are not really separable; he can be both witty and lyrical, almost at one and the same moment. This strange and perfect blend of characteristics apparently so incompatible makes Aristophanes a wonderful man to read, and we begin to understand why Plato loved the old rogue as he did; he must have been a wonderful man to know.

2

Profiles · in · History

The Legacy of the Elizabethans and Jacobeans

Christopher Marlowe: Inspirational but Raucous Rogue

Philip Henderson

Born into a quarrelsome family in Canterbury, England, Christopher Marlowe (1564–1593) carried with him a propensity to fight that colored his short life and may have led to his untimely death from a stab wound. Some scholars, however, argue that Marlowe, who was suspected of being a spy during his college years because of some lengthy, clandestine absences, was actually assassinated. Young Marlowe attended some of the finest schools in England, including Corpus Christi College in Cambridge. In spite of his rowdy nature, he excelled in Latin verse and over a five-year period immersed himself in the lifestyle of a bohemian writer, producing such plays as *Doctor Faustus*, *The Jew of Malta*, and *Edward II*. Marlowe's work was well known and respected in England, and young William Shakespeare was greatly inspired by him.

In this excerpt from his book *Christopher Marlowe*, author Philip Henderson profiles Marlowe's life and his poetic and dramatic works, most of which were published

Philip Henderson, *Christopher Marlowe*. London: Longmans, Green & Co., 1956. Reproduced by permission of the author.

posthumously. Henderson also wrote *Tennyson: Poet and Prophet* and *Algernon Swinburne: The Portrait of a Poet.*

❧   ❧   ❧

A good deal more is known about Christopher Marlowe, for good or ill, than about any other dramatist of the Elizabethan Age. Since the discovery in 1925 of the inquest proceeding after his death, followed in 1929 by Professor F.S. Boas's *Marlowe and His Circle*, the balance of interest in recent critical studies has tended to shift from his work to his life. More is known about Marlowe chiefly because his name occurs fairly frequently in academic, secret service and police records—or their equivalent in his day. But we do not know enough to form a complete picture of him, though the psychological criticism of our own time has inferred much. Evidently, in his brief, tragic and passionate life, Marlowe was the kind of man who could not help making enemies and letting off squibs *pour épater le bourgeois* ['to flabbergast the middle class']. He seems to have lived, as he thought, dangerously.

In a now famous phrase, Mr. T.S. Eliot once described Marlowe as 'the most thoughtful, the most blasphemous (and, therefore, probably the most Christian) of his contemporaries'. To his contemporaries, however, he appeared in a different light. His fellow playwright Robert Greene attacks him, in his *Groatsworth of Wit*, as an epicure, an atheist and a Machiavellian. Nevertheless, it was Marlowe, with his intellectual passion and his over-reaching Machiavellian hero-villains, who indicated the direction of subsequent Elizabethan tragedy. . . .

The eldest son of a well-to-do tradesman, a shoemaker of some local standing, Christopher Marlowe was baptized at St. George's Church, Canterbury, on 26 February 1564—exactly two months before the baptism of William Shakespeare at Stratford-upon-Avon. Both poets came from the same stratum of society—the rising middle-class. Marlowe was entitled to call himself a gentleman by virtue of his Cambridge degree, Shakespeare by virtue of a newly-established coat of arms. Both poets, by their genius, won the patronage of the great. Shakespeare managed his affairs so well that on his death he was commemorated by a bust in his parish church: Marlowe lies in an unmarked grave at Deptford. In contemporary records his name appears variously spelt: Marley, Morley, Marlin, Merlin, Merling. Both he and his father signed themselves Marley, though the baptismal register reads 'Christofer the sonne of John Marlow'. From King's School, Canterbury, he went up in December 1580 to Corpus Christi College, Cambridge, on a scholarship founded by Matthew Parker, former Archbishop of Canterbury and Master of Corpus. The scholarship was for six years and was granted more or less on the understanding that those holding it should study for the Church. 'Merling', however, first appears in the college records as a student of dialectics.

Outwardly Marlowe's academic career was uneventful, except for mysterious and increasingly long absences after his second year. During his last year, in 1587, it needed the intervention of the Privy Council before the University would allow him to take his M.A. degree. For it appeared that not only had Christopher Marlowe given up all idea of going into the Church, but it was rumoured that he intended to join Dr. Allen's Catholic seminary at Rheims. As it was, the Privy Council assured the worried University authorities that 'in all his actions Christopher Morley had behaved himself orderly and discreetly whereby he had done Her Majesty good service'. The despatch concluded: 'Because it was not Her Majesty's pleasure that any one employed as he had been in matters touching the benefit of his country should be defamed by those that are ignorant in th'affairs he went about'. The despatch is dated June 1587. . . . It is not known whether Marlowe's government service was confined to carrying despatches to and from ambassadors and courts abroad, or whether he was also one of [spymaster] Francis Walsingham's spies. The likelihood is that he did work as a spy.

A Master's Degree Is Awarded

Needless to say, with such powerful backing, Marlowe took his M.A. degree in July 1587, and before the end of the year both parts of *Tamburlaine the Great* had been performed on the London stages. He was now twenty-three. He had had six years at the University and now had another six years in which to complete his work. During that time he wrote five or, possibly, more plays, *Hero and Leander*, and translations [of works by Ovid and Lucan]. . . . During the remaining six years of his life he lived chiefly in London, in the theatrical district of Shoreditch, though he may have travelled a good deal on government commissions. In September 1589 he was imprisoned in Newgate for his part in a street fight in which the son of a Holborn publican was killed, and appeared for trial together with Thomas Watson, the poet and playwright, at the Old Bailey on 3 December. He was discharged with a warning to keep the peace. This he failed to do, for three years later he was summoned to appear at the Middlesex Sessions for assaulting two Shoreditch constables in Holywell Street. The constables said that they went in fear of their lives because of him. But there is no evidence that Marlowe ever answered this particular charge. In the early part of 1592 he appears to have been at the siege of Rouen

[France], where English troops had been sent to uphold the Protestant cause against the Catholic League, for on 12 March a 'Mr. Marlin' arrived at Dieppe with a letter from the English garrison at Rouen to Sir Henry Unton. From Dieppe Unton sent him back to England with a letter to Lord Burghley. *The Massacre at Paris*, Marlowe's most topical play, shows such an intimate knowledge of French politics, that it was probably written soon after these events. Its hero-villain, the Duke of Guise, was the same Guise whom the chivalrous Unton challenged three times to single combat to answer his insulting references to Queen Elizabeth I.

In the autumn of this year appeared Robert Greene's *A Groatsworth of Wit*, attacking both Marlowe, as the 'Famous Gracer of Tragedians', and Shakespeare as 'the Upstart Crow beautified in our feathers'. Some of Greene's most scandalous charges against Marlowe were cut out by Henry Chettle [the playwright who arranged the publication of the pamphlet]. These, said Chettle, 'at the perusing of Greene's book . . . I thought he in some displeasure writ; or had it been true, yet to publish it was intolerable. With neither of them that take offence was I acquainted, and with one of them I care not if I never be'. This was evidently intended for Marlowe, for Chettle makes handsome amends to Shakespeare.

Next year, in May 1593, Thomas Kyd, the dramatist, was arrested and examined under torture for having in his possession heretical papers 'denying the deity of Jesus Christ', which he said belonged to Marlowe and had been accidentally shuffled among his own 'waste and idle papers'. As a result of this, on 18 May, Marlowe was summoned to appear before the Privy Council and, on the 20th, 'commanded to give his daily attendance on their Lordships until he shall be licenced to the contrary'. Such summonses were not unusual and Marlowe was neither imprisoned, nor treated as a suspected person—though Kyd, as a scrivener [scribe], had been suspected of writing the 'mutinous libels' set up in the Dutch Churchyard against the refugee French and Flemish weavers. Twelve days later Marlowe was killed in a tavern at Deptford, the famous dockyard adjoining Greenwich.

The Death of Marlowe

Marlowe's death has given rise to more speculation than anything in his life. But the various theories advanced to account for it raise more problems than they settle. Lately, however, they have reached their apotheosis in Mr. Calvin Hoffman's contention that Marlowe was not killed at all, but lived on in exile and wrote all the plays and poems attributed to the actor Shakespeare. Returning to established fact, we know that three days before Marlowe was killed at Deptford by Ingram Frizer, an informer Richard Baines laid before the Privy Council a *Note containing the opinion of one Christopher Marly concerning his damnable judgement of religion and scorn of God's word.* The horrified informer concluded his long list of Marlowe's blasphemies with a demand that 'the mouth of so dangerous a member may be stopped'.

Marlowe's reported table talk is of two kinds, one consisting of blasphemies which Christians in any age will find horrible—such as 'that Christ deserved better to die than Barabbas' and 'that if the Jews among whom He was born did crucify Him they best knew Him and whence He came'—and, on the other hand, a rationalistic criticism of the Scriptures, such as is now known as the Higher Criticism. The most dangerous indictment was that he was in the habit of saying that 'the first beginning of religion was only to keep men in awe' (which he seems to have got from Machiavelli) and that 'almost into every company he cometh he persuadeth men to atheism, willing them not be afeard of bugbears and hobgoblins'. There are also references to such subjects as the age of Adam ('That the Indians and many authors of antiquity have assuredly written above sixteen thousand years agone, whereas Adam is proved to have lived within six thousand years'), the poor literary style of the New Testament (that he could have written it much better) and that Moses made the Jews travel for forty years in the wilderness, 'a journey which might have been done in less than one year', in order that those 'who were privy to his subtleties might perish, and an everlasting superstition remain in the hearts of the people'. To these dangerous speculations Marlowe added a plea for homosexuality and smoking—smoking being at that time a new and revolutionary practice, more or less confined to [English navigator, historian, and poet Sir Walter] Ralegh and his immediate circle. In fact Ralegh is directly involved in Marlowe's reported saying that 'Moses was but a jugler, and that one Herriots [Thomas Harriot], being Sir Walter Ralegh's man, can do more than he'. Baines's charges are substantiated by Kyd's letters to Sir John Puckering, written after Marlowe's death, and in *Remembrances of words and matter against Richard Cholmeley*, which also names Ralegh as having heard 'the atheist lecture'. Though Marlowe evidently took a fiendish delight in shocking his contemporaries, one can still see behind the Baines Note a keenly humorous and scientific mind at work. . . .

Judgement and Remembrances

Marlowe's death was hailed triumphantly by the Puritan pamphleteers as a manifest instance of God's judgement upon 'a filthy playmaker', an atheist and a blasphemer. . . . [George] Peele wrote of 'Marley the Muses' Darling'; [George] Chapman said that he stood up to the chin in the Pierian flood; [Thomas] Nashe—who also wrote an *Elegy on Marlowe's Untimely Death*, which appeared in some copies of the first edition of *Dido*, none of which now survive—spoke of 'poor deceased Kit Marlowe'. Only Kyd, who had got into trouble because of him, said that he 'was intemperate and of a cruel heart' and in the habit of 'attempting sudden privy injuries to men'. The best epitaph was written by Michael Drayton in the next century:

> . . . Marlowe, bathed in the Thespian springs,
> Had in him those brave translunary things
> That your first poets had; his raptures were
> All fire and air, which made his verses clear,
> For that fine madness still he did retain
> Which rightly should possess a poet's brain.

In truth, Marlowe differed from his contemporaries not so much in degree as in kind. He was, said [Algernon] Swinburne, 'the most daring and inspired pioneer in all our poetic literature; the first English poet whose powers may be called sublime'.

Plays and Poems

Only one of Marlowe's plays, the first and second parts of *Tamburlaine the Great*, was published in his lifetime. This appeared anonymously in 1590. Next to appear, in 1594, the year after his death, were *Edward II* and *Dido, Queen of Carthage*, which carries Nashe's name as well as Marlowe's on the title page. No collected edition of the plays appeared, and the result is that their texts vary from the comparative goodness of *Tamburlaine* and *Edward II* to the varying degrees of corruption of *The Massacre at Paris* and *Doctor Faustus*, of which the last two Quartos survive, the 1616 version being almost twice as long as that of 1604. Marlowe's texts suffered the fate of all very popular plays in that age, mauled and maltreated by the players and periodically polished up by some theatrical hack. But fragmentary as they mostly are, it is by no means certain that this is not something very like the state in which he left them. We cannot, that is, blame everything upon inferior collaborators and the corruption of texts, and the very temper of the man himself may survive in the spasmodic brilliance of his work.

Marlowe's plays held the stage right into the middle of the next century, till the Puritans closed the theatres. Edward Gayton in his *Pleasant Notes Upon Don Quixote* (1651) tells us that on holiday afternoons, and especially at Shrovetide [the three-day period preceding Ash Wednesday], an audience composed largely of sailors, watermen, shoemakers, butchers and apprentices would force the players to act their favourite pieces—'sometimes *Tamerlane*, sometimes *Jugurth*, sometimes *The Jew of Malta*, and sometimes parts of all these. . . . And unless these were done . . . the benches, the tiles, the laths, the stones, the oranges, apples and nuts flew about most liberally'. Since then *Tamburlaine* has been regarded as unactable till Donald Wolfit and Tyrone Guthrie produced a shortened version of both parts at the Old Vic, London, in 1953. Sickening as the experience was, it left no doubt at all of Marlowe's mastery of theatrical effect.

William Shakespeare: The Bard of Stratford-upon-Avon

A.A. Mendilow and Alice Shalvi

The body of dramatic works by William Shakespeare (1564–1616) remains unrivaled in the frequency with which the plays are still performed today. Since the time of Elizabethan England, when "the Bard" thrilled Londoners with his tragedies, histories, and comedies, a fascination has swirled about the Bard of Stratford-upon-Avon who wittily and poetically penned so many masterpieces, including the tragic *Romeo and Juliet*, the timeless *Henry VIII* and *Hamlet*, and the comedic *The Taming of the Shrew*. Shakespeare's life was the stage, and ultimately the actor-playwright held a share in the Globe Theatre south of the Thames River and even had his own company of actors.

In this excerpt from *The World and Art of Shakespeare*, authors A.A. Mendilow and Alice Shalvi piece together the life of Shakespeare from baptism, marriage, and death records; registries of plays and poems; references in books, diaries, letters, and journals; and from his own writings and choices of themes and imagery. Mendilow headed the English department at Hebrew University in Israel from 1948

A.A. Mendilow and Alice Shalvi, *The World and Art of Shakespeare*. Jerusalem: Israel Universities Press, 1967. Copyright © 1967 by the Israel Program for Scientific Translations. Reproduced by permission.

until he retired in 1973. His main areas of teaching and publishing were the novel and romantic poetry. The author of *Time and the Novel,* he died in 2000. Shalvi is professor emeritus of English literature at Hebrew University. Her specialties remain Shakespeare and drama. She is the author of *Renaissance Concepts of Honour in Shakespeare's Problem Plays* and *Women in Israel.*

🔹 🔹 🔹

'Time, which antiquates antiquity' has left Shakespeare untouched, as fresh and alive as when he wrote. He serves as the touchstone of taste for every generation, and the best key to the aesthetic beliefs of every school of writing and criticism since his day is the different way he has been interpreted by each. . . .

Shakespeare was born in 1564—the exact date is unknown. The traditional date of April 23rd started in the eighteenth century, and seems to derive from two sources. April 23rd is the day of St. George of Lydda, the Patron Saint of England (his painting riding a horse and fighting a dragon was on the wall of the Guild Chapel in Stratford); Shakespeare died on April 23rd, 1616. Such coincidences, however attractive, are unproved. All that is certainly known is the date of his baptism, April 26th, 1564, exactly 2 months after the baptism of his great predecessor and model in drama, Christopher Marlowe, and some ten weeks after the birth of another herald of a new world concept, Galileo. Shakespeare was baptised in the church of the Holy Trinity in Stratford, then an important country town in the heart of England, where his father, who came from a nearby village, had established himself as a prosperous tradesman and leading citizen. Shakespeare's mother came from an old Catholic family of small land-owners in the vicinity of Stratford. His father too may have been brought up as a Catholic in his youth, a common occurrence in the early part of the sixteenth century, before the new Church of England finally asserted its predominance in the consciences of the people. It was John Shakespeare who in 1561 gave instructions as a town official to remove signs of Catholic ritual from the Guild Chapel on the coming of Queen Elizabeth to the throne. Nevertheless, it was perhaps these Catholic origins that gave rise to a statement by a clergyman at the end of the seventeenth century that Shakespeare died a Catholic. Though there are no grounds for such a belief, and though he was baptised into the Church of England, his mother's Catholic connections may account for the lack of anti-Catholic prejudices in his writings at a time when such prejudice was common. His priests, friars and cardinals are sympathetically portrayed, but they expound no specifically Catholic doctrines.

His Father's Disappearance from Public Life

In 1565, Shakespeare's father became an Alderman, and in 1568 the High Bailiff or Mayor of Stratford. In the latter year, and again in 1569, when Shakespeare was four and five years old, two companies of actors from London performed at Stratford, and were officially entertained by Shakespeare's father. In 1576 he was Justice of the Peace and Chief Alderman of the town. By 1578, however, he seems to have lost much of his money and could not meet his bills and taxes; he sold some of his wife's property and mortgaged the rest, though, since he retained possession of three houses in Stratford, he cannot have been utterly impoverished. From 1587 to his death in 1601, whether because of poverty or for some private reason one cannot be certain, he apparently no longer held any public office in the town in whose government he had served in so many capacities for a score of years. William was the third of eight children, his two elder sisters both dying in childhood, and the eldest of five sons. According to tradition and by inherent probability, he was educated at the Stratford Grammar School which provided free education for sons of the burgesses of Stratford such as Shakespeare was. Its academic standing was high, and the teachers were graduates of Oxford and very well paid in comparison with most other schools. The teaching there consisted mainly of Latin grammar and a number of Latin classics, and Shakespeare's writings show his familiarity with the standard authors and texts of the normal grammar school curriculum. The bible in its English translation of the mid–sixteenth century, known as the Genevan version, was also studied, and in the higher classes—rhetoric. Shakespeare's friend, the classical scholar and playwright Ben Jonson wrote after Shakespeare's death that he knew 'little Latin and less Greek'. By modern standards, Jonson's 'little Latin' would mean quite a good grounding in the language and literature, but it is true that Shakespeare later preferred to rely on translations of Latin authors; of a knowledge of Greek his writings show no evidence at all. There is an amusing scene in *The Merry Wives of Windsor* (Act IV, Scene 1) in which a schoolmaster examines a boy in his lessons, and this offers a picture of the kind of education to which Shakespeare was subjected. He was probably withdrawn early from school owing to his father's impoverishment or disgrace or whatever it was that caused him to leave public life, and later tradition supports this assumption of an early break in his schooling. How he spent his youth is not known. Various legends have come down, all late and contradictory: that he was apprenticed to a butcher; that he taught at a school, etc. Conjectures have been made that he studied law, that he became a soldier, that he travelled abroad, and so on, but these are quite unfounded. Nothing whatsoever is definitely known of his occupation till 1592, by which time he was in London as an established actor and had already started to write plays.

Marriage to Anne Hathaway

The facts known about Shakespeare's earlier life are these: On November 27th 1582, when he was eighteen years of age, the application was recorded of a special license to marry Anne Whateley without waiting for the usual banns [proclamations of an intended marriage]. Such applications though uncommon were not rare, and were often connected with the long periods of the year when for religious reasons no marriages could be performed. The following day, bonds were given to allow the license to be granted to marry Anne Hathaway, the daughter of a yeoman and about eight years older than her betrothed. Though the groom was a minor, the two sureties to guarantee the ecclesiastical authorities against any claims arising out of the license were hers, not his. The name Whateley may have been a clerk's error or may hide some romance. The place and exact date of the marriage are unknown, but some six months later, on May 26th, 1583, a daughter Susannah was baptized in Stratford, the child of William Shakespeare and his wife, formerly Anne Hathaway. In 1585, their twins Hamnet and Judith, named after a Stratford baker and his wife who were friends of Shakespeare, were baptised, but the boy died in 1596. No more children were born to them. It is conceivable, though not certain, that advice given in *Twelfth Night* may be the outcome of his own experience: 'Let still the woman take an elder than hersel'; likewise the warning in the *Tempest* that pre-nuptial intimacy breeds 'barren hate, sour-eyed disdain and discord'.

There is good reason to believe that Anne came from an orthodox Puritan family. If so, this may possibly explain why she did not accompany her husband to London but remained in Stratford, since the Puritans were bitter in their hatred of the theatre and the acting profession. Be that as it may, for nearly twenty years, Shakespeare lived alone in hired lodgings in London, whereas every other member of the theatrical company to which he belonged, except for two who remained bachelors, were householders in London where they lived with their families. Shakespeare visited Stratford periodically, and in the course of his working life he bought considerable property there, finally retiring to his native town at the end of his life. How and where Shakespeare spent his time before 1592 is then unknown, though later traditions have tried to fill the gap in our knowledge. He may have been the William Shakeshafte (a variant of the name used by Shakespeare's grandfather) who is recorded in 1581 as a private player in the service of a Lancashire gentleman. Did he join one of the four companies that performed in Stratford in 1587? There is no way of knowing. His first biographer, Nicholas Rowe (1676–1718), dramatist and editor of Shakespeare's plays in 1709, records a tale that he stole a deer from the estate of a neighbouring landowner and wealthy Member of Parliament, Sir Thomas Lucy. The story goes that Shakespeare was prosecuted and punished so severely that, after composing an insulting ballad on Sir Thomas, he had finally to escape to London. Unfortunately for the story, the Lucy family had no deer park on their estate at that time. Other legends relate that he started his career in London at an unspecified date as a callboy or as an actor in minor parts or by looking after the horses of visitors to the theatre during the performances. All that we know for certain, however, is that by 1592 he was sufficiently famous as an actor and playwright to serve Robert Greene (1558?–1592, novelist, dramatist and pamphleteer) writing on his deathbed, as one against whom to warn his friends, who being like him University graduates looked on dramatic writing as their monopoly: 'there is an upstart Crow, beautified with our feathers, that with his *Tygers hart wrapt in a Players hyde*, supposes he is as well able to bombast out a blanke verse as the best of you: and being an absolute *Iohannes fac totum* ['a jack of all trades'], is in his owne conceit the onely Shake-scene in a countrey.' In view of the parody of a line from an early play of Shakespeare and of the hidden pun in 'Shake-scene', the probability is strong that it was Shakespeare who was the object of Greene's attack. An apology for this attack was made by another minor playwright Henry Chettle (1560?–1607?) who had arranged for the posthumous publication of Greene's pamphlet; in this, he testified to the admirable character of the maligned person and to his skill and reputation both as actor and writer.

Poems for a Nobleman

In 1593 and 1594, during which years the London theatres were closed because of the prevalence of the plague, there appeared in print Shakespeare's two long narrative poems, *Venus and Adonis* and *Lucrece*, each dedicated to the Earl of Southampton, a young nobleman of Catholic antecedents. He may have been the young nobleman whom Shakespeare in the sonnets urged to marry and found a family. Southampton was also the patron of Florio, the author of the Italian-English dictionary and translator of [French essayist Michel de] Montaigne's Essays. Shakespeare drew on the translation in *The Tempest*, II, i. Florio married the sister of the poet and dramatist Daniel whom Shakespeare knew and who may have been the rival poet of the Sonnets. Davenant, Shakespeare's godson, stated that Southampton had given his godfather a very large gift of money, namely one thousand pounds. The figure stated is clearly impossible, and this detracts from the reliability of the source, but there is the possibility that a gift of some money enabled Shakespeare to gain financial security by buying a share in a leading theatrical company, as he indeed did in 1594. Putting hypotheses and traditions aside, we know that in that year he became a member of a theatrical company under the patronage of the Lord Chamberlain, and his name was recorded as one of those receiving payment for acting in plays at court the following winter. Thereafter, a number of his plays were noted in the Stationers' Register, or referred to as having been acted at Court or in the public theatres, and many of them were printed. In 1598, a clergyman and schoolmaster named Francis Meres (1565–1647) mentioned twelve of his plays, his poems and his sonnets, and referred to him as outstanding in comedy and tragedy, and noteworthy for sweetness of diction. 'As the soule of *Euphorbus* was thought to live in Pythagoras: so the sweete wittie soule of *Ovid* lives in mellifluous and honytongued Shakespeare, witnes his *Venus and Adonis*, his *Lucrece*, his sugred Sonnets among his private friends, etc. As *Plautus* and *Seneca* are accounted the best for Comedy and Tragedy among the Latines: so Shakespeare among the English is the most excellent in both kinds for the stage. . . . As *Epius Stolo* said, that the Muses would speake with *Plautus* tongue, if they would speak Latin: so I say that the Muses would speak with Shakespeare's fine filed phrase, if they would speak English'.

The 'sugred Sonnets' did not see print till 1609, however. Meanwhile, evidence appears of Shakespeare's growing prosperity. In 1596, his father renewed an application for a grant of arms for which he had applied in 1568 but had abandoned. This grant, which made him a 'gentleman', was duly issued the same year, and in 1597 Shakespeare purchased one of the finest houses

The plays of William Shakespeare, many of which were based on events in England's history, were popular with the public and the royal court alike.

in Stratford for sixty pounds. This remained in the family till the death of Shakespeare's last descendant, his granddaughter Lady Bernard, in 1670. He was also in friendly contact with a fellow townsman, whose son was later to marry Shakespeare's daughter Judith, and who paid him the compliment of asking him for a loan of a large sum of money, namely thirty pounds. In 1598 he was one of a syndicate of seven actors who transferred the theatre set up in 1576 by [actor James] Burbage, and called The Theatre. The new building South of the river Thames was the famous Globe Theatre, and Shakespeare had one tenth share in the venture, the two sons of Burbage having one half between them. In that year, he acted in Ben Jonson's play *Every Man in his Humour*, and the two were thereafter close friends. At this time he was living in Bishopsgate, London, but by 1599 he had moved to the South bank of the Thames, outside the City, but near his theatre. In 1602, he bought considerable land near Stratford for £320.

When Queen Elizabeth died in 1603, Shakespeare's company of actors, the Lord Chamberlain's Men as they were known, were taken over by the new King, James I. Shakespeare is not mentioned in any of the lists of actors after 1603, but in 1608 he was still referred to as a player by one of the Burbage brothers. As he was one of the leading share-holders of the company, and as his play-writing and possibly overseeing the production of them may have been considered as an equivalent of the acting duties of the other members he probably did less acting than the other members of the company who were listed as performing at Court after 1603. From a lawsuit in which he appeared as a witness in 1612 it appears that in 1604 he was lodging with a Frenchman, a Huguenot wig-maker, in London. He must have been highly regarded, for he was entrusted with negotiating the marriage settlement of the daughter of the house to an apprentice. In 1605, he bought for £440 some local fixed rents. In Stratford, his eldest daughter married a local doctor in 1607, and in due course gave birth to a daughter. His father had died in 1601, and his mother in 1608. One brother became an actor and died in 1607, while two other brothers died in 1612 and 1613 in Stratford. His sister had married in Stratford too.

Back to Stratford

Shakespeare retired to Stratford probably in 1610, but he still visited London from time to time, and continued to write or collaborate in writing plays. After 1613, when he bought a house in London for £140 which he immediately mortgaged, he seems to have given up all active work. His last recorded visit to London was in 1614. On April 23rd, 1616, after a short illness William Shakespeare of Stratford-on-Avon, Gentleman, died. Half a century later, a local clergyman entered in his diary a story he had heard that 'Shakespear, [Michael] Drayton, and Ben Jonson had a merry meeting, and itt seems drank too hard, for Shakespear died of a feavour there contracted'. Drayton was a leading poet and dramatist who came from nearby, while Jonson was the dramatist who wrote the famous verses to Shakespeare that prefaced the First Folio, the first collected edition of the plays, published in 1623.

In his will, drawn up a month before his death, Shakespeare remembered many of his old theatrical colleagues as well as several friends in his home town. His wife is not mentioned in any of the bequests, but by law she was entitled automatically to the income of one third of the property for life; as an after-thought she was also left the second-best bed. This afterthought may be interpreted as confirming the hypothesis that the couple were not happy together, or as underlining Shakespeare's romantic love for his wife in leaving her the bed they themselves had used. The bulk of the property was bequeathed to his daughters and their heirs, but the last grandchild died in 1670, no descendants were left, and the line became extinct. Shakespeare was buried inside Stratford church, and a doggerel verse on the stone above his grave cursing anybody who disturbed his body prevented the exhumation of his remains to make room for later inmates, as was then the custom. The graveyard scene in *Hamlet* gains in poignancy when one remembers Shakespeare's desire to be left in peace. Some years after his death, a bust of the dramatist was placed on the wall near his tomb in the church; it was made by a professional tomb-maker of the time and can still be seen. How far it resembles the poet we cannot tell, but it presumably satisfied the family. His wife died in 1623, in the year when the collected works of Shakespeare were published in the magnificent volume known as the First Folio as a memorial to him by his fellow-actors.

Ben Jonson: Noted Playwright with a Satiric Tongue

Henry G. Lee

Ben Jonson (1572–1637) wrote London-based satires that gained him recognition as a literary leader in England while at the same time earning him enemies and landing him in jail more than once. Besides sedition and slander, he was accused of such crimes as treason and murder.

Jonson probably first met William Shakespeare when the latter's company performed Jonson's play *Every Man in His Humour* in 1598, and the two became friends. Jonson is best known for his humor comedies, in which he instilled in each character a human foible, and for his innovations to the masque, the principal form of performance—colorfully incorporating dance, music, speech, and scenery—produced for the royal court of James I.

In his introduction to Jonson's *Volpone, or The Fox*, Henry G. Lee takes a look at the life of the playwright and how, despite his inclination to stir up trouble, he rose to be honored for his poems and plays. Lee is professor emeritus of the School of Communications and Theater at Temple University in Philadelphia.

Henry G. Lee, "Introduction," *Volpone, or The Fox*, by Ben Jonson. San Francisco: Chandler Publishing Company, 1961. Copyright © 1961 by Chandler Publishing Company, renewed in 1989. Reproduced by permission of Pearson Education.

❦ ❦ ❦

In [the twentieth] century, Ben Jonson is probably the best-known of Elizabethan playwrights excepting, of course, [William] Shakespeare, and perhaps, [Christopher] Marlowe. However, very few people in our day have read his plays, and, unfortunately, fewer still have had the occasion to see his work performed in the theatre. Yet in Elizabethan times no one was more famed than Jonson; he was crowned with honors and tributes in his final years (including an honorary degree of Master of Arts from Oxford) and was buried in pomp in Westminster Abbey in 1637. To be sure, this contemporary fame was not entirely the result of his work in the theatre. He was also important as a poet and his contributions to the highly specialized and now-departed semi-dramatic masque form were distinguished and successful.

But Ben Jonson, the man, was perhaps more responsible for his own reputation than any of his literary works. In an age which produced an efflorescence of fascinating characters and notorious individuals, Jonson, whether by accident or design, seems to have made the Elizabethan equivalent of the headlines as regularly as the most publicized movie star of today. On at least seven occasions of record, he was hauled before the courts or the authorities on various charges ranging from sedition and treason to murder, frequently in connection with cases attracting wide public attention. His participation in the "War of the Theatres" early in his career brought him notoriety among the intellectuals of the time and the piercing satire of his plays brought reaction from individuals and groups who saw their follies exposed to public view. His indomitable ego brought him into conflict with many important people and made him many enemies. His well-known artistic feud with the great court designer, Inigo Jones, continued off-and-on for almost thirty years and thus his controversial personality was exposed in the limelight of the royal court.

He was, in short, a well-publicized full-blooded example of the breed of English Renaissance individualists. He reached his position of eminence from extremely humble origins by reason of great intellect, aggressive drive, and, above all, open integrity. He could, for example, never succumb in public or in private to the use of flattery as a politic device. If the honored French Cardinal Duperron made a bad translation of [the Roman poet] Vergil, Jonson had to tell him directly "that they were naught," even if this churchman did happen to be the current lion of the French literati. The same kind of candidness breathes from the pages of his great stage satires.

Modest Beginnings

Jonson's story is the familiar tale of the rise to greatness from humble origins. He was born about 1572, in the London which was to be his home for the rest of his life and the locale for most of his plays. He was the son of a poor clergyman who died shortly after the boy's birth. He attracted the attention of William Camden, headmaster of Westminster, one of England's best schools. To Camden he owed his introduction into the world of scholarship and his knowledge of the classic authors. This start was important to a future writer who lacked the means for a university education and had instead to apprentice himself to his stepfather's bricklaying trade. Boredom led to Jonson's enlistment as a volunteer in the army then fighting in Flanders [a country in northwestern Europe in medieval times]. A fine physical specimen and an excellent swordsman, he went off to seek adventure on the field of battle. But he found, as so many young men in [the twentieth] century have found, that military life even in wartime can sometimes be very dull and uneventful. So he sought out an enemy, met him in single combat in the presence and under the observation of both armies, and disarmed and killed his opponent; then, having made his mark in war, he quit the military life and returned home to challenge fame in another way.

But life was hard in Elizabethan London for a young writer who had no connections and no wealth. The professional theatre beckoned. The second Golden Age of drama was beginning to flourish and at least six public theatres already existed in or near London. William Shakespeare, another man of humble beginnings, only 33 years old, had already wrung enough profit from the theatre to buy a country estate. Jonson joined a company of strolling players and quickly rose into star parts, most notably as the hero of Thomas Kyd's tingling thriller, *The Spanish Tragedy*. He came to the attention of the astute manager, Philip Henslowe, who recognized not an actor, but a playwright. Jonson was put to work finishing *The Isle of Dogs*, an abandoned play by Thomas Nashe. When produced, it was judged to be seditious and slanderous. Jonson and two of the actors were imprisoned in a widely advertised case.

When released from prison, Jonson again went to work writing for Henslowe, but his first major successful comedy and the beginning of a long line of brilliant satires was produced in September, 1598, not by Henslowe but by the Lord Chamberlain's Men with Shakespeare in the cast. *Everyman in His Humour* was an immediate success and introduced a dramatic technique which Jonson himself labeled as a "comedy of humours." In the same month, Jonson, in an argument of unknown cause, killed one of Henslowe's actors. He escaped the gallows, but lost all his goods by confiscation and was branded on the thumb.

Pen as Sword

A series of plays for several different companies followed. Jonson's satirical gibes at his fellow playwrights, whom he considered careless and more interested in popular success than in quality, resulted in a series of plays known as the "War of the Theatres," in which playwright attacked playwright, and through which Jonson's vitriolic pen became famous. The "war" culminated in 1601 with the free-swinging comedy *Poetaster*, in which Jonson ridiculed not only such popular playwrights as John Marston and Thomas Dekker, but also took aim at actors, soldiers, and the legal profession.

The accession of James I to the throne of England in 1603 was a signal event in Jonson's life. James was a ruler intensely interested in literature and scholarship and the playwright enjoyed the patronage of the court through most of James' twenty-two year reign. In 1603, also, appeared Jonson's first major tragedy, *Sejanus*. It was a pronounced departure from the series of realistic "humour" comedies of London life with which he had first made his mark. The new play was based on Roman history and hewed to the stern and formal lines of classic tragedy. It failed. It also incurred the wrath of the Earl of Northampton, who charged "popery and treason," although Jonson seems to have escaped punishment.

The next year Jonson collaborated with his erstwhile literary foe, John Marston, and with George Chapman, in the writing of a bustling London satire, *Eastward Ho!* The play contained some sharp slurs on the Scots which were construed as an attack on the new king. Back to jail went Jonson together with his fellow "culprits," but the intervention of influential persons accomplished his release. In spite of his outspoken candor, an apparent personal magnetism made many important friends for Jonson throughout his life.

Fit to Write for a King

An incident at court in 1604 illustrates Jonson's penchant for frankness. He apparently made some disparaging remarks about the court masque of this season, which had been written by one of his rivals. As a result, he was expelled from the court for "unmannerly behavior." But King James apparently recognized the truth of the criticisms, for in 1605 Jonson began his long association with the court entertainments which resulted in a series of superlative masques and elevated the form to literary significance. The masque was a traditional entertainment composed of song and dance. During the Renaissance in Italy and France it had undergone a metamorphosis into an elaborate and expensive show, which integrated music, dance, rhetorical speech, and spectacular scenery. It was the principal medium of court entertainment for such celebrations as royal weddings and the Twelfth Night revels. Jonson's important contributions to the form included the raising of the dialogue into poetry of quality and the invention of the antimasque, a kind of contrasting section of antic nature introduced into the usual formality of the masque structure. Jonson's collaborator was the great architect and designer, Inigo Jones, who had studied the masque form in Italy. From the beginning, their collaboration was marked by contention. Jonson saw the masque as an opportunity for literary expression; Jones saw it as the ideal medium for scenic and spectacular display. Their association was stormy.

Jonson continued writing for the public stage. *Volpone* was first acted by Shakespeare's company at the Globe in the early months of 1606, and later in the same year received performances at Oxford and Cambridge. It was followed by three other great comedies, *Epicoene* (1609), *The Alchemist* (1610), and *Bartholomew Fair* (1614). These four plays compose the portion of the playwright's work which is best known and respected in our time and which reached a new peak of quality in English comedy.

By 1614 Jonson was the recognized leader of literary England. The magnet for most of the outstanding younger writers of the day, he was also the close friend of such major figures as [Sir Walter] Raleigh, [John] Donne, [John] Milton, and [Sir John] Suckling. He continued to contribute to the court masques, but his later plays were of minor importance. His death was widely mourned and his burial at Westminster Abbey was attended by most of the gentry and the literary great of England.

Jonson was the powerful advocate of the classic tradition in an age which was frequently willing to forget the niceties of literary creation and which often sacrificed integrity and care to the demands of speed and superficial effect. He believed with the classic writers that the function of poetry was to delight *and to instruct.* He demonstrated the classic virtue of "sticking to the point," of maintaining a unity of subject and action. Furthermore, his plays deal, as did the classic dramas, with the truths of life, with what is typical in human action and character. However, Jonson's power rests partly in the fact that he was no servile imitator of the classic authors. He used classic principles to build a contemporary comedy based squarely in the life of his own time. He was no ivory-towered scholar dreaming of Greece and Rome, but, as his life attests, a lusty participant in his own exciting age. He thus gave to English comedy a full measure of integrity and craftsmanship without compromising the vital energy and richness and variety of realistic detail so characteristic of the drama of the Elizabethan age.

Unique Comedic Style

Everyman in His Humour and its sequel, *Everyman Out of His Humour*, established his comic view as vastly different from Shakespeare's and [Robert] Greene's romantic versions of the comic spirit. Using caricature as a major mode of characterization, he built up a *dramatis personae* in which each character embodied a particular human foible, a special observable "humour" in human beings. He then proceeded to invest these types with a classically detailed and integrated plot which exposed the follies of each to laughing ridicule. From the beginning, Jonson's "comedy of humours" was a critical comedy.

That his aim was good and his delineation of the "humours" precise is well demonstrated by the troubles he incurred from individuals who saw themselves in his stage portraits. The very specificity of these characterizations, however, tends to dilute their effectiveness with following generations, and the "humour" plays of Jonson have long since disappeared from our stages. Once a folly has been chastised and corrected, the instrument of chastisement is no longer necessary.

In *Volpone* and the other great plays of the later period, Jonson turned to more universal human traits for his subject matter, and these plays have enjoyed a much longer life. The subject of *Volpone* is greed, and greed is a human folly that seems not to have diminished with the passage of time. The subject is as valid for our own materialistic age as it was for Jonson's and *Volpone* remains his most popular play.

CHAPTER

3

Profiles · in · History

Eastern Poets Stage Vivid Performances

Guan Hanqing: Portrayer of Yuan China

James M. Hargett

During the Yuan dynasty, Guan Hanqing (also known as Kuan Han-ch'ing, ca. 1220–ca. 1300) rose to prominence among his contemporaries in what has been called the golden age of Chinese drama. Although China was invaded and occupied by the Mongols, the cities grew and the dramatic arts flourished. Guan penned more than sixty plays, including comedies and melodramas, and he explored numerous themes: historical and military, love and marriage, and courtroom story lines. He strove to portray realistic characters, developing men and women who broke the molds of commonality.

In the following piece from *Great Literature of the Eastern World*, James M. Hargett discusses Guan Hanqing's place in the history of drama and his artistic priorities. He also takes a look at various dramas to gain further insight. Hargett, who holds a PhD from Indiana University, is an associate professor in and has served as chairperson of the East Asian studies department at the State University of New York at Albany. His area of specialization is the Song dynasty.

❦ ❦ ❦

Guan Hanqing is China's best known and most prolific playwright. He lived during the Yuan (Yüan) dynasty (1260–1368), a time when China was invaded and
occupied by foreign conquerors—the Mongols. This
was the same period in which Marco Polo (c. 1254–
1324) visited the Middle Kingdom. Despite the presence of alien rulers, the theater flourished in China under Mongol rule. The spectacular growth of cities at this
time provided a fitting environment for all sorts of entertainment, especially dramatic performances. These
urban centers in Yuan dynasty China were directly responsible [for] the rise of the *zaju* (*tsa-chü*) drama, a theatrical form in four acts that consists mainly of dialogue
and arias. Although this "golden age of Chinese drama,"
as it is so often called, produced a host of outstanding
playwrights, none occupies a more preeminent position
than Guan Hanqing. More than 60 plays are attributed
to his authorship, some 21 of which are extant today.
Fifteen of these works are complete and include several
comedies and melodramas, one farce, and at least two
works that might be called tragedies. The remainder
survive only in partial or fragmented form.

Guan Hanqing's productivity and exalted status as
the "father of Chinese drama" notwithstanding, few
facts are known about his life. Scholars agree on only a
few minor details of his biography: Guan was a native
of Yanjing (later known as Dadu) in north China (modern Beijing); he once visited Lin'an, the capital of the
Southern Song (Sung) dynasty, sometime after its fall
to the Mongols in 1276; and he lived to an old age.
Virtually every other surviving account or anecdote related to his life and career is controversial and thus un-

reliable. His extant plays, however, provide ample material to describe and define Guan's skill as a dramatic artist.

Guan's Artistic Priorities

The most distinguishing feature of Guan Hanqing's plays is the vivid picture they reveal of Chinese society under Mongol rule in the thirteenth century. A close reading of his extant works strongly suggests that Guan had two artistic priorities. First, he was most interested in portraying characters who are convincingly real and believable on stage. Guan Hanqing loathed one-dimensional, stereotypical characters such as women bound by rituals and behaviors designed by men (examples include the obedient young maidservant, the dutiful wife, the loyal widow, and so on). He also avoided common plot lines such as that of the young scholar, bound for the capital to take the civil service examinations, who encounters obstacle(s) on the road, eventually overcomes these impediments, and wins first-place in the examinations. Instead Guan sought to achieve an atmosphere of realistic portrayal that mirrors the complexities of life in Yuan dynasty China, which helps to explain the general lack of supernatural miracles common to the works of many of his contemporary Yuan playwrights. Moreover, Guan generously mixes seriousness and humor to illustrate "positive" (filial piety) and "negative" (overblown vanity and pride are among his favorite targets) modes of behavior in his characters.

As for his second artistic priority, although Guan Hanqing undoubtedly wrote dramatic works that were designed for performance and entertainment, like virtually all Chinese authors, he also created characters and story lines intended to instruct his audience. This didactic purpose of his plays always features the diametrically opposed forces of "good" (a paragon of moral virtue) and "evil" (an oppressor of the common people) in conflict with one another. Without exception, the forces of good eventually overcome those of evil.

Dramatic Themes

Although one could discuss Guan Hanqing's plays in a number of ways, a convenient and useful approach is by theme. This is because most plays written in China during the Yuan period fall into easily identifiable thematic categories, two or more of which often overlap in the same play. The most popular of these concern the following: love and marriage, religion and supernatural happenings, history/military and pseudo-historical/military figures and episodes, family and social situations, murder and courtroom drama, and bandit-hero adventures. . . .

[One] general theme in Guan's *Works* is love and marriage. This is a common topic in Chinese literature, and is usually portrayed in a sterile and highly stylized manner. For example, in many (if not most) Yuan plays, young unmarried women are portrayed as "prizes" won by successful examination candidates. Rarely do we find a serious and complex character portrait of a woman. In Guan Hanqing's works, however, there is no shortage of such characters.

In *Rescued by a Coquette (Jiufeng chen/Chiu-feng ch'en)*, a play considered by many to be one of the best Yuan dynasty *zaju* comedies, Guan brilliantly portrays a battle of wits between a sing-song girl (that is, a prostitute-entertainer) and the powerful, evil son of an official. The playwright's ultimate purpose is to reveal the innermost thoughts and desires of the sing-song girl, who, as it turns out, is not lascivious and greedy but, like many women, interested in love, marriage, and security. Not only does the sing-song girl Zhao Paner (Chao P'an-erh) emerge as a crafty and worthy opponent to the profligate young official, but her wit, intelligence, and courage make her a genuine heroine.

Another female lead, Tan Qier (T'an Ch'i-erh), appears in *The Riverside Pavilion (Wangjiang ting/Wangchiang t'ing)*. In this work we again encounter an intelligent and courageous heroine pitted against a worthless but mighty male rival—Lord Yang. After having Tan Qier prevail over her opponent, Guan Hanqing addresses the question of her widowhood. Although widows were strongly discouraged from remarrying in ancient China, Guan Hanqing allows Tan Qier to take a second husband. The playwright's description of their romantic love is unmatched in Chinese literature. . . .

Among Guan Hanqing's plays dealing with justice and trials, *Injustice to Dou E (Dou E yuan/Tou O yüan)* undoubtedly provides the most drama and greatest emotional appeal. The plot line of this and other "courtroom" dramas is similar: early on in the play the protagonist is wrongly accused of a crime and unjustly punished (execution is the usual form of punishment). The remaining acts focus upon retribution and the redress of wrongs, which is usually brought about in a courtroom scene by a wise judge, a bandit-outlaw, or supernatural intervention.

In the case of *Injustice to Dou E*, Dou E is a young widow who dutifully lives with and serves her mother-in-law. Their tranquil and uneventful world is suddenly shattered, however, with the arrival of two evil suitors, to whom the mother-in-law is indebted for saving her life earlier. The mother-in-law is willing to marry the older suitor, but Dou E—still faithful to her husband's memory and filial duty to her mother-in-law—steadfastly refuses. The younger suitor then decides to get rid of the mother-in-law (to "free" Dou E), but his plot goes awry and his accomplice is poisoned instead. Dou E is thereupon dragged off to court where she is forced to confess to killing the suitor, is sentenced to death, and then executed. Later, with the assistance of some timely divine intervention, the case is reopened, Dou E is exonerated posthumously of her guilt, and the villain is duly punished.

Throughout the play, but especially in the arias, Guan Hanqing elevates Dou E as a person of tremendous moral courage who, despite pain, torture, and even death, remains true to the virtues of chastity and filial duty. Her character is also appealing because she is a "mere" commoner who is unrelenting in her fight against oppression in a morally corrupt society. In the end, justice is won, but only after the innocent are forced to endure much suffering. Ultimately, Guan Hanqing's emphasis is on the moral lesson: though the good and innocent are often crushed by evil oppressors, all villains—regardless of their social station—are eventually held accountable for their crimes.

Zeami Motokiyo: Perfecter of Japanese Nō Theater

J. Thomas Rimer

Zeami Motokiyo (1363–1443) is most often associated with the Japanese theater of Nō, a uniquely expressive form that relies on music, dance, and poetic language and uses no scenery, few props, and only male actors. Zeami credited his father, Kan-ami, with creating Nō, but it was Zeami who took the theatrical style to its highest level. He learned the dramatic form as a child actor in his father's troupe, which traveled the country performing at festivals, and upon his father's death, the twenty-two-year-old Zeami stepped in and took over the administrative reins of the troupe while still acting, writing, and theorizing.

In his piece on Zeami from the *Critical Survey of Drama: Foreign Language Series*, J. Thomas Rimer chronicles the playwright's life and describes the poetic world of Nō. Rimer is on the faculty of the East Asian language and literature department at the University of Pittsburgh in Pennsylvania.

J. Thomas Rimer, "Zeami Motokiyo," *Critical Survey of Drama: Foreign Language Series*, edited by Frank N. Magill. Englewood Cliffs, NJ: Salem Press, 1986. Copyright © 1986 by Frank N. Magill. All rights reserved. Reproduced by permission.

🐒 🐒 🐒

$\mathbf{A}$s a young man, Zeami [Motokiyo] took the popular theatrical forms available to him as an actor, and through his education, the force of his will, and his insight into the theatrical process, he mastered a highly disciplined and poetic theatrical form, the Nō, which not only became the central focus for the highest traditions in the Japanese theater of his period, but also became the model and the touchstone for all the developments that followed in later centuries. In a very real way, Zeami and his dramas remained a source of inspiration for poets and playwrights up to the twentieth century. Not only did later writers of the Nō continue to emulate his methods of composing plays, but Kabuki and puppet dramatists from the seventeenth century onward borrowed plots, characters, and settings from Zeami's Nō dramas, often as a gesture of homage to the man whom they regarded as the greatest dramatist in the entire Japanese tradition. In the twentieth century as well, there [was] new interest in the work of Zeami. Modern Japanese dramatists such as Yukio Mishima have rewritten some of the old plays, finding in them the seeds of a contemporary consciousness, and Western writers and musicians from William Butler Yeats and Paul Claudel to Bertolt Brecht and Benjamin Britten have taken sustenance from these works to create their own modern versions of the Nō. For modern Western playwrights, Zeami, read in translation since the 1920's, seemed the first and perhaps the greatest exponent of a form of total theater that combined text, movement, gesture, dance, music, and chant into one transcendental unity. Other practitioners of the Nō, notably Zeami's father Kan'ami, began to approach this synthesis, but only Zeami fully attained it. For the modern Western reader, Zeami's dramas have a particular power in their concentrated poetic language that, even in translation, makes these plays uniquely able to suggest a dramatic movement from the world of everyday understanding to the realm of the ineffable. No other writer in the long Japanese tradition of the Nō possessed quite this power of language. In this aspect of his work, Zeami, however gifted as an actor, singer, and theoretician, was truly singular.

Zeami's Career

Despite the fact that Zeami Motokiyo was famous in his lifetime, relatively little is known about him. This is partially because, in his time, actors had very low social status. In fact, without the help of powerful patronage, Zeami might never have received the level of literary training one needed to learn the canons of Japanese poetry, which figure so heavily in the aesthetics of his dramaturgy.

Zeami began his career as a child actor in the troupe of his father Kan'ami (1333–1384), who took his troupe to shrines and temples for performances at festivals all over the country, staging his plays for a variety of local patrons. When Zeami was a boy of twelve, the shōgun Ashikaga Yoshimitsu (1358–1408), the political ruler of the nation and a powerful patron of the arts, saw his performance and was so captivated by the beauties of Zeami's technique as well as his person that he decided to patronize Kan'ami's troupe and have Zeami educated properly. It is clear from reading Zeami's treatises, written in his mature years, that he had become extremely well versed in the arts of poetry, literature, and philosophy, subjects to which a low-ranking person such as an actor could normally expect to have no access whatsoever.

Zeami's father died when the young actor was only

twenty-two, and Zeami spent the rest of his career as head of the theatrical troupe which his father had led, serving as administrator, actor, playwright, and theoretician. As long as the patronage of Yoshimitsu continued, Zeami enjoyed high favor; when Yoshimitsu's successor Yoshimochi took power, however, Zeami began to lose favor in the court. In 1428, when Yoshimochi's younger brother Yoshinori became shōgun, Zeami and his family began to suffer real hardships. Eventually, at age seventy-two, Zeami was exiled to the remote island of Sado. Tradition has it that he was pardoned and permitted to return to the capital shortly before his death in 1443, but details concerning these matters are conflicting and obscure.

Zeami Motokiyo wrote a considerable number of plays. Many, but not all, of the texts survive. Because of Zeami's importance in the history of the Nō, and of the homage always paid him, a large number of plays have been generously ascribed to his hand. Modern scholarship has lowered the number considerably. Judicious cross-referencing in the various treatises written by Zeami suggests a total of between forty and fifty plays which can safely be attributed to him.

It is also extremely difficult to date the individual texts, since accurate performance records do not exist from that time, and since his plays were often restaged, given new titles, and partially rewritten by Zeami himself. In his treatises, Zeami always recommended in performance a juxtaposition of the old and the new, in order to stimulate, but not to bewilder, an audience, and he often adapted even his best plays to suit new circumstances of performance.

The Uniqueness of Nō

The dramatic form which Zeami perfected, the Nō, differs considerably from any Western form of drama.

Perhaps the closest Western analogy might be chamber opera, where music and text intertwine, yet the parallel is inexact, since the Nō involves masks and elaborate costuming, no scenery, only male actors, a few props, and a crucial use of dance. Even in musical terms, the score of a Nō play would be considered as partially improvised, with the orchestra and chorus following the lead of the chief performer. Thus, reading the text of a play by Zeami is a process similar to reading an opera libretto, which suggests, but does not re-create, the whole. Unlike many libretti, however, the Zeami texts reveal poetry of striking, synthetic beauty. For such modern Western writers as Yeats and Claudel, Zeami had achieved a form of poetic drama that seemed fully complete in itself. . . .

Visions of Poetic Worlds

The form of a Nō play, as developed by Zeami and discussed at length in his treatises, uses a particular structure which is repeated (as are various musical and dramatic aspects found in traditional operatic form) in most of the plays. A Nō drama might best be described as a vision. The skill of the playwright lies in his ability to lead his audience into that vision. The figures presented and the poetic worlds conveyed may change, but the means by which the vision becomes possible on the stage must remain the same. Usually a particular play begins with the arrival of a priest or other traveler, who comes to a spot that has a history: a place where a famous person has lived or died, a crucial battle was fought, or a noted poet has found inspiration. Opened to the experience of the place by his own knowledge and sympathy, the traveler next meets a person, often a rather mysterious one, who, through conversation, ascertains that the traveler is indeed one who has the ability and the sympathy to grasp the real meaning of what has happened there. Often this section of a Zeami play is couched in elegant and poetic language, so the first encounter is followed by an interlude in which a rustic or some other similar character repeats the nature of the incident; in this way, everyone in the audience can grasp the significance of the encounter. Then, in the final section of the play, the mysterious person whom the traveler first met reveals his or her true nature and describes in grand poetic language the event that happened on the spot, re-creating the moment also in dance, song, and mime. The play, which has begun slowly, reaches its highest pitch, then concludes as the vision fades and the newly enlightened priest or traveler, along with the audience, once again finds himself in the real world.

Zeami did not invent the form of the Nō; indeed, he credited his father with the first high accomplishments in the genre. Nevertheless, it was in Zeami's hands that the potential of the form was fully realized, and in all five categories of Nō drama, Zeami's work constitutes an unsurpassed standard. Zeami often adapted plays by other writers; perhaps his greatest achievement is the reworking of a text presumably composed by his father; Zeami's play is entitled *The Wind in the Pines*. This piece is a "woman play" about the love of two fisher-girls, Matsukaze and Murasame, for a courtier from the capital, Ariwara no Yukihira (818–893), who was exiled at Suma Beach, where the play takes place. In *The Wind in the Pines*, every element of Zeami's art combines to form a unified poetic whole. . . .

Enduring Dramatic Expressions

Despite the variety of tonality and subject matter, all [of Zeami's] plays . . . have certain strong philosophical and emotional resemblances. The pain and chagrin of passion remembered, the growth of an understanding that salvation lies beyond and not in this world, and the sav-

ing power of a sincere emotion all link the dramas of
Zeami to the sort of Buddhist philosophy prevalent in
Japan during the difficult political period in which he
lived. The confusion and disappointments of secular
society at this time were such that a withdrawal in
search of some transcendental understanding of reality
became an important possibility for many people before, during, and after Zeami's generation. Such attitudes thus provided a logical point of departure for the
characters that the playwright created for his audiences.
Yet the kind of emotional self-consciousness that Zeami
posited in those characters seems to make them accessible as well (though initially in radically different ways)
to modern readers and audiences who may, for quite
different social, political, and personal reasons, feel
themselves alienated from society. It may be links such
as these that make the work of Zeami seem strikingly
contemporary. Even modern readers and spectators
find that Zeami's work touches and justifies their most
private feelings, showing by remote example something
about the human condition that is wholly recognizable.
In the end, Zeami's powerful belief in the efficacy of
poetry, as Yeats was the first Westerner to observe,
comes through as clearly today as when these dramas
were first composed and performed.

Rabindranath Tagore: An East Indian Who Touched the World

Saranindranath Tagore

Calcutta-born Rabindranath Tagore (1861–1941), a Renaissance man in his own time, left an enormous body of literary works—plays, poems, novels, essays, and short stories—that have been translated from Bengali for much of the world to enjoy. This brilliantly talented man from India was surrounded by a family of highly accomplished individuals. In 1913 Tagore reached a pinnacle of his own, receiving the Nobel Prize in Literature. But his achievements did not end there; he also wrote close to two thousand songs and, in later life, produced hundreds of paintings.

Tagore had an impact on politics and education as well, for a time taking a lead role in world affairs and later establishing the Visva-Bharati University in Bengal.

In this excerpt from *Rabindranath Tagore: Final Poems*, Saranindranath Tagore shares the many facets of his relative's life. Saranindranath Tagore is the great-grandson of artist Abanindranath Tagore, the nephew of Rabindranath Tagore. He is an associate professor in the philosophy department at the National University of Singapore. His cur-

Saranindranath Tagore, "Introduction," *Rabindranath Tagore: Final Poems*, selected and translated from the Bengali by Wendy Barker and Saranindranath Tagore. New York: George Braziller, 2001. Copyright © 2001 by Wendy Barker and Saranindranath Tagore. All rights reserved. Reproduced by permission.

rent research interests focus on Indian philosophy, European philosophy, and the works of Rabindranath Tagore.

 ❦   ❦   ❦

Rabindranath Tagore (1861–1941) is one of the greatest cultural figures of modern India. He was born into a Calcutta family that was at the forefront of the political and social renaissance that shaped the life of the city in the nineteenth century. Rabindranath's grandfather, Dwarkanath Tagore, was a leading Indian entrepreneur with diversified business interests. He tirelessly sought to support his friend Rammohan Ray in his numerous reform efforts such as the banning of the institution of widow immolation. Rabindranath's father, Debendranath, is regarded as one of the great architects of the new Hinduism and is a towering figure in the history of Indian religious thought. Rabindranath's older brother, Jyotirindranath, was a composer, a dramatist, and a translator of literature from European languages. His sister, Swarnakumari Devi, was a novelist of great originality. His nephews, Abanindranath and Gaganedranath, are two great figures in the history of modern Indian art.

Born into such an illustrious family, Rabindranath's life is studded with achievements that are astonishing in their breadth and scale. As a writer, he was a poet, a novelist, a short-story writer, an essayist on a rich diversity of topics, a dramatist who produced and acted in his own plays, and a lifelong writer of magnificent letters. He was also a composer of almost two thousand songs called *Rabindrasangīt* that created an entirely new style within Indian musical traditions. Rabindranath, in fact, is the only composer in the world whose songs stand today as the national anthem of two independent nations: India and Bangladesh. At the age of seventy, he started to doodle with erasures in his manuscripts that gradually evolved into paintings. In the last fifteen years of his life he produced more than a thousand paintings that are startling in their bold experimentation. His brilliance did not stop at the literary, the musical, or even the artistic; he was also a participant and leader in the social and political affairs of the world. In 1905, when the British divided Bengal into East and West Bengal, Rabindranath was at the helm of a protest movement called Swadeshi. He retired from active participation in politics when the movement turned violent. Building on this experience, he later wrote the novel *Home and the World* (adapted for the screen by Satyajit Ray) where, through the character of Nikhil, Rabindranath elaborated a social philosophy that [University of Chicago Law School professor] Martha Nussbaum has recently called cosmopolitanism. Never hesitant to act on his beliefs, Rabindranath renounced his knighthood in 1919 as a protest against the Massacre of Amritsar perpetrated by the British. Perhaps the greatest achievement of Rabindranath as a man of action was the establishment of Visva-Bharati University in rural Bengal. In this institution, with its motto "the world in one nest," Rabindranath sought to build an educational program founded on the principle of international cultural exchange. He was perhaps the first educational thinker in the modern world who put into practice the notion that a complete education must be open to the diverse cultural heritages of the world. Figures such as Indira Gandhi (former prime minister of India), Satyajit Ray (world-renowned filmmaker), and Amartya Sen (Nobel Prize–winning philosopher-economist), among others, are products of Rabindranath's educational institution and philosophy.

World Recognition

While preparing to visit England in 1912, Rabindranath fell ill and had to cancel the trip. Convalescing in rural Bengal, he took to translating into English some of the religious poetry that he had recently published in Bengal. Eventually, he made the trip to England later in the same year and presented some of the English versions in a reading that was attended by a group of eminent cultural figures of London, including [poet] William Butler Yeats. A limited edition of these translations, *Gitanjali*, was published in London the same year with an introduction by Yeats. While Rabindranath in 1912 was already the leading literary figure in the Bengali language, he was almost unknown in the West. In 1913, only a year later, he was awarded the Nobel Prize in literature and became a world figure virtually overnight.

The world fame of Rabindranath in the post–Nobel Prize period of his life rested in part on translations made into many of the languages of the world. After *Gitanjali*, upon the insistence of his English publisher, Macmillan, Rabindranath himself produced several volumes of translations of his works. Most of the translations into other languages, both in Europe and Asia, were made from these English versions. In both these regions, Rabindranath remains to this day an important literary presence. The 1999 *Time* magazine poll of the twenty most influential Asians of the twentieth century includes Rabindranath as the only literary representative. The influence of his works continues to proliferate in some parts of the world because great writers translated him: Juan Ramón Jiménez, Anna Akhmatova, André Gide, among others. They produced compelling presentations of Rabindranath's work (in Spanish, Russian, and French, respectively), even though these versions were made from the English editions, which did not sustain the power of Rabindranath's original Bengali. In the Anglophone world, however, there are no equivalent examples of powerful translations of Rabindranath's work for much of the twentieth century. Fortunately, more recently, a new generation of translators have taken up the challenge of re-presenting Rabindranath to the English-speaking world. In the 1980s and 1990s, William Radice, Ketaki Kushari Dyson, Krishna Dutta, and Andrew Robinson have contributed to the renewal of interest in Rabindranath by publishing some exciting volumes of translations made from the original Bengali. . . .

Indian writers who write in English are now celebrated. And rightly so: they are indeed fine writers. It is a mistake, however, to think that the handful of novels produced by this group exhaust the modern Indian literary tradition. The great literary traditions in the languages of India must be included in any understanding of modern Indian literature. In this respect, the achievements of Rabindranath Tagore are pivotal. Apart from his profound impact on the development of Bengali literature, his writings deeply influenced the modern literary traditions in the other languages of India as well. Rabindranath is indispensable to the reader interested in Indian literature.

We speakers of the Bengali language are always conscious of Rabindranath's legacy; for us the language as we know it is inconceivable without his writings. The Bengali believe that in Rabindranath's writings, especially in his poems and songs, every nuance of the human condition is recorded. In the Anglophone world, however, Rabindranath was stereotyped as a mystical poet, partly because the first wave of translations following the Nobel Prize concentrated only on his deeply theistic poems. Any one selection cannot do justice to the immense variety of poetry that Rabindranath wrote throughout his life. . . .

Writings on Death

The consciousness of death . . . was sadly all too present in the poet's life. In a series of tragedies, he lost his three children and wife. As the youngest of fourteen siblings, he bore the loss of most of his brothers and sisters. These harrowing experiences of recurring grief found expression in the poetry and song of the Tagorean oeuvre; in his work, the immense healing power of resignation is the one source of deep and lasting consolation. The poetry of *Gitanjali*, which captured the imagination of the West, evokes some of these grief-stricken moments, which none of us are spared. . . .

The consoling power of Rabindranath's writings on death led Janusz Korczak, the legendary Polish educational thinker and activist, to produce Rabindranath's play *The Post Office* with the children of his orphanage in the Warsaw Ghetto. Two months later, Korczak and the children were taken away and gassed in Treblinka. When asked why he chose to stage *The Post Office*, Korczak reportedly responded by saying "because eventually one had to learn to accept serenely the angel of death."

In his final poems, written after a major illness and with death beckoning, Rabindranath gives us in words the movement of his thoughts as *he* approaches death. There is no raging against the dying of the light, only an unadorned honesty intermittently lit by luminous memories.

4

Profiles · in · History

Europeans Pen the Social and Political

Molière: Comedic Critic of French Society

H. Ashton

Molière (Jean-Baptiste Poquelin, 1622–1673), a Parisian-born playwright, actor, and troupe manager, used comedic and farcical dialogue in his plays to criticize aspects of French society. The dramatist sparked quarrels and made powerful enemies with his play *Tartuffe*, or *The Imposter*, which agitated the religious community and was temporarily banned by the Catholic archbishop. He was also accused of attacking individuals, including other writers, through thinly veiled caricatures in his dramas. Molière's controversial work did not diminish his popularity with King Louis XIV, however, who asked Molière to entertain in his court.

In this excerpt from *A Preface to Molière*, author H. Ashton chronicles Molière's life: his decision to follow his own aspirations against his father's wishes, his early days playing the provinces, his battle with other dramatic troupes in Paris, his successes and failures, and his dramatic death. Ashton, who died in 1952, was a professor at the University of British Columbia and a fellow of the Royal Society of Canada.

H. Ashton, *A Preface to Molière*. Folcroft, PA: Folcroft Library Editions, 1927.

Jean Baptiste Poquelin, later known as Molière, was born in Paris in 1622. The entry of his baptism shows clearly the social standing of his family. "On Saturday, 15 January, 1622" it reads, "was baptized Jean, son of Jean Pouquelin, and of Marie Cressé, his wife, living in the Rue St. Honoré: godfather, Jean Poquelin, grain-porter (grandfather): godmother, Denise Lescacheux (Marie Cressé's grandmother) widow of the late Sebastien Asselin, upholsterer."

Molière was the first-born of a family of bourgeois, or middle-class Parisians, people of some fortune, living comfortably: when his mother died (ten years later) the inventory of the family possessions shows their fortune to have increased, the shop to be well stocked, their furniture good, their clothes and linen of the best quality, and their silver and jewellery of considerable value. A few years earlier Molière's father had purchased the office of court upholsterer and *valet de chambre* to the King [Louis XIII]. A year after the death of Molière's mother his father married again. By this marriage there were two children, one of whom died soon after birth, and a few days after the death of this child the mother also died. Molière's father was left with a family of five children. We know little of the boy's stepmother and of his early life. Legend has it that his grandfather (Cressé) took him for walks in the Paris streets and even to the theatre but it is difficult to find any real authority for these stories.

What we do know is that by careful management of business, by economy and sober living the family increased its fortune and improved its social standing by the purchase of a position at court. It is easy to see where Molière learned his lessons of common sense and caution. But it is not sufficient to know one class of society. Born a bourgeois, Moliére was able to study the people in the populous quarter in which he lived in Paris; and at court and in the shop he early became acquainted with nobles. He received the usual education of a bourgeois—first at school in Paris, then at the Faculty of Law at Orleans, was called to the bar but appears to have practised law little, if any. It is frequently stated that he also studied philosophy with [French scientist, mathematician, and philosopher Pierre] Gassendi in Paris, but it is difficult to see how he could have done this during the time he resided there.

The education he received was a sound classical training—the equivalent, now-a-days, of a good Arts course, with some legal knowledge in addition. This should be remembered when one reads descriptions of the wandering actor who later wrote great comedies. Molière had a better education than many of his contemporary critics.

Father and Son at Odds

If his father had planned to educate his son so that he could rise above the ranks of the bourgeois and enter the *noblesse de robe*, as lawyer-nobles were called, he was soon to be grievously disappointed. Jean Baptiste declared that the call he heard was not to legal honours but to the stage. Much has been written on the quarrels that ensued between father and son and it were well to examine, for a moment, the reasons for this misunderstanding.

The father certainly objected to his son's entering the career he had chosen and this is not surprising when one remembers that acting was not yet a profession. Poquelin had evidently intended to improve the social standing of his son. Qualified for one of the most honourable professions, the one that might most easily raise a bourgeois to the ranks of the nobility and, incidentally, permit him to amass a fortune, Molière was deliberately sacrificing everything by going on the stage. Naturally his father did not immediately concur in this. Efforts have been made to improve the situation by stating that Molière was to join a troupe of young nobles—a sort of aristocratic Players' Club. This is nonsense. A glance at the list of actors who signed the first contract with Molière is sufficient to convince us that his father had some cause for uneasiness. The names are: Beys, Poquelin, Bonnenfant, M. Béjart, G. Béjart, J. Béjart, Clerin, Pinel, Malingre, Desurlis. The Béjarts were near neighbours of the Molières and Madeleine [Béjart] was a professional actress and a woman with a past. The others were all of very humble origin.

When Molière's father saw that his son could not be turned aside from the theatre, he appears to have done all he could to help him financially. The new troupe assumed the title of "The Illustrious Theatre" but it was unable to convince Parisians that it was really illustrious. Before very long it was so deeply in debt that Molière found himself in prison. His father again came to his aid.

Playing in the Provinces

After this catastrophe Molière left Paris and became a member of a troupe of strolling players and later the "manager" of a similar troupe. We know little about his life between 1645 and 1659. He played in the south of France and at Lyons and the places visited include Toulouse, Albi, Carcassonne, Nantes, Narbonne, Agen, Grenoble, Lyons, Montpellier, Avignon, Pézenas, Bordeaux, Béziers and Rouen. He returned to Paris in 1658. While this period of his life is little known it is one of the most important in his career as a dramatist. It extends from his twenty-fourth to his thirty-sixth year, brings him a wide and varied experience of life at an age at which he could profit by it, teaches him the craft of acting and what the public expected of the stage. "He who goes down among the people, or into the provinces," says [French moralist Jean de] La Bruyère, "soon makes strange discoveries if he has eyes, sees things there that he would not have expected and of which he could have not the least suspicion; he advances by repeated experiences in knowledge of human beings." No one can read Molière's plays without recognizing how much he owes to this long and fruitful apprenticeship in the provinces.

It was immediately after this experience that Molière made a most important discovery. At Paris, in the early days, and during his wanderings in the provinces he seems to have imagined that he was a tragic actor. During his peregrinations his troupe produced many tragedies but, little by little, his reputation was established by his amusing plays. He certainly wrote farces while on tour and soon after his return to Paris he gave himself to the playing of farce and comedy. *L'Etourdi* [*The Scatterbrain*] and *Le Dépit Amoureux* [*A Lovers' Quarrel*] date from this provincial period.

Molière had travelled north to Rouen to get into touch with a friend who had promised to introduce him at court. He had evidently decided that the moment had arrived to conquer Paris as he had so rashly set out to do long before. Years of training and experience had built up for him in the provinces an enviable reputation and he returned with every hope of success, but with a modesty and tact that came from the buffeting of the world. Thirty-six years of age, mature in thought and in stagecraft, he re-entered Paris as leader of a troupe of actors who had the protection of the King's [Louis XIV] brother [Philippe I] and who appeared in October, 1658, in the Salle des Gardes of the Royal Palace, the Louvre. They produced a tragedy with qualified success, for the audience was used to the actors of the Hôtel de Bourgogne, who played with pomp and dignity if not with bombast. After the tragedy Molière begged leave to play before His Majesty one of his little comedies that had been favourably received in the provinces. There was no doubt as to the success of this and he was commanded to establish his troupe in Paris.

A Rivalry of Troupes

It must not be assumed that Molière—just because he was Molière—became at once the hero of the day. He was, as yet, merely a strolling player who had dared come from the provinces to perform before Parisians. He found three troupes in possession of the field. The Italians used the hall—the Petit Bourbon—that the King had allotted to him and he had to pay them an indemnity for the expense to which they had been put when they installed their theatre. Nor did he then enter into complete possession. He could play only alternately with them and he had to leave them the most popular days—Tuesday, Friday and Sunday.

The second troupe—the Théâtre du Marais—was not "protected," as was Molière's by the King's brother, and it had fallen on evil days after the death of its greatest actor, Mondory, and the desertion of others. While it still had an occasional success it was not likely to cause Molière much uneasiness.

The real rival was the third troupe—the Hôtel de Bourgogne. This was the Royal Troupe, pensioned by the King, privileged to use special placards for its plays, the favourite of the public, able to obtain the best tragedies from the great playwrights of the day and openly scornful of the Bohemian band from the provinces that had the impertinence to stage the same plays as they performed.

Molière settled down in Paris, not to day-dream of

success, but to make friends, to ensure agreement among the members of his troupe, to replace with good actors those who withdrew, or who died, to provide suitable plays and to act them as well as possible. Within a year the Italian troupe left the field for a time and Molière immediately changed to the more popular days of the week, and on November 18, 1659, he had his first great success with *Les Précieuses Ridicules* [*The Affected Young Ladies*].

He had definitely opened his campaign of social criticism and therefore added to his professional enemies of the Hôtel de Bourgogne others who considered that their mode of life was criticized in the play. There followed a "quarrel of the *Précieuses*" as there was to be later a "quarrel of the *Ecole des Femmes* [*The School for Wives*]" and a "quarrel of *Tartuffe*.". . .

A Struggle to Emerge

From this time onwards the life of Molière is largely the story of his successes and failures, his play-writing, his struggles with his enemies, his steady progress to a higher type of comedy and to the undisputed place he holds among the great writers of the world.

In January, 1661, the troupe took possession of the finest theatre in Europe—the Palais Royal. Competition, instead of decreasing, was again becoming more acute and there were soon six companies of actors in Paris. The play intended to establish Molière as a great writer—*Don Garcie de Navarre* [or *The Jealous Prince*]—was a failure. The disappointment was keen and he hastened to produce a different type of work, *L'Ecole des Maris* [*The School for Husbands*], a real comedy with but little of the farce element that was, at first, so evident in his comedies. It was a complete success and, when it was published, Molière dedicated it to his patron Monsieur, the King's brother.

Not content to rest upon his laurels, he produced immediately *Les Fâcheux* [*The Bores*]. It succeeded and Molière had therefore nothing to fear from the Italian actors who returned to share his theatre with him. As newcomers, however, they were forced, this time, to take the less popular days of the week that they had formerly allotted to Molière. A week after their return the successful actor manager, then aged forty, married Armande Béjart, the youngest sister of that Madeleine Béjart with whom he had set out on his theatrical career. She was only twenty years of age.

Armande became a member of her husband's troupe and it continued a very successful season during which *L'Ecole des Femmes* was produced. The brilliant success of this play awakened the jealousy of Molière's enemies and to them he replied in *La Critique de L'Ecole des Femmes* and *L'Impromptu de Versailles*. The attacks came from all quarters but Molière seems to have taken seriously only one of them, that accusing him of representing well-known persons at court. This was, of course, equivalent to a statement that his characters were not creations from wide experience but caricatures of individuals and that accusation Molière would not permit. Nor could he afford to make such bitter enemies at court as would have been any individuals so attacked. His replies were well received but, though the quarrel continued with increased bitterness, he declined to take any further part in it and chose the wiser course of quietly going on his way.

Entertainment for the King

The King called upon him frequently to prepare entertainment for his court but even when busy with pieces written to order Molière seems to have kept in view the more important studies of the society of his day. Soon after *Le Mariage Forcé* [*The Forced Marriage*] and the rapidly prepared *Princesse d'Elide* [*The Princess of Elida*] he played before the King three acts of a new play *Tartuffe*.

This gave rise to a quarrel that lasted nearly five years and created for its author some very powerful enemies. The first attack came from a religious association known as *Compagnie du Saint-Sacrement* which had sufficient influence to obtain from the King an order forbidding the production of the play in public. Molière continued to read it and even to play it in private, and the fact that the King tolerated this, in view of the opposition that it aroused, and that he tolerated it even in houses at which he was visiting at the time, proves that he sympathized with the author. In 1667 he permitted a public performance of the play but, immediately afterwards, the King being absent from Paris, the influence of the *Compagnie du Saint-Sacrement* again prevailed and the play was banned by the Archbishop. The successful authorization by the King did not come until late in the following year.

This period must have been a particularly trying one for Molière. Not only had he to fight for his play, *Tartuffe*, and checkmate his enemies, but he had also to bear the burden of personal bereavement. In 1664 two of his best friends died and at the end of the year he lost his eldest son. In spite of all this he was working on *Le Misanthrope* [*The Misanthrope*] and he rapidly prepared and produced *Dom Juan* [*Don Juan*]. This play aroused a storm of disapproval, again for religious reasons, but Molière refused to reply to his detractors, dropped *Dom Juan* from his repertory and persisted in his efforts to free *Tartuffe* for the public.

He had not lost the King's favour as a result of the quarrel but became his appointed entertainer, and one of the first commanded plays, proposed, written, learned and produced in five days, had the temerity to represent on the stage four well-known physicians. This appears to be the first occasion on which Molière deliberately indulged in personalities—from which he always steadfastly maintained that he was free—but as the performance was a private one for the court only he may have been of the opinion that no exception would be taken.

Supremacy at Last

In 1666 appeared another of his great comedies, *Le Misanthrope*, and from this moment his place as the greatest writer of comedy of his day and his place in the King's favour were definitely assured. While there were still three well-known plays to come from his pen (*Le Bourgeois Gentilhomme* [*The Bourgeois Gentleman*], *Les Femmes Savantes* [*The Feminine Savants*] and *Le Malade Imaginaire* [*The Imaginary Invalid*]) his struggles for supremacy were over and we may pause, for a moment, to ask ourselves whether the King's favour was an unmixed blessing.

To Molière's knowledge of the provinces, of the bourgeois of Paris, of the people, it added familiarity with the court. It protected him from powerful enemies who might, otherwise, have compassed his downfall. On the other hand it called him away from serious work to prepare court entertainments of an ephemeral nature and his life became a round of activity. . . .

There is, in the archives of the *Comédie Française* in Paris, a document of primary importance for the history of Molière's troupe—a manuscript register kept by the actor La Grange. On a Friday in February, 1673, La Grange noted the first performance of a play entitled *Le Malade Imaginaire*, and, in the margin, he added, "New and last play of M. de Molière." It was, indeed, while playing the part of the man who imagined he was ill that Molière was seized with a fit of coughing and broke a blood-vessel. He was carried to his home in the Rue de Richelieu and died during the night. As Molière, like other actors, was excommunicated by the church his widow had to appeal to the King to obtain permission to have him buried by night in consecrated ground.

Henrik Ibsen: Norwegian Realist

Kenneth McLeish

Norwegian-born Henrik Ibsen (1828–1906) is sometimes called the father of modern drama because of his divergence from drama written in verse to prose drama. During his most productive years, spent in a self-imposed exile in Italy, Germany, and Denmark, he moved from historical themes to plays that addressed social ills and later on to the use of mysticism and symbolism in his work. A couple of his most popular plays, *A Doll's House* and *Hedda Gabler*, deal with marital conflicts over gender roles.

In his introduction to Ibsen's *Peer Gynt*, Kenneth McLeish provides an overview of Ibsen's life journey, including his twenty-seven years outside of Norway, and the major works he produced. McLeish translated most of the well-known Greek playwrights and some Romans. Other translations were from playwrights Ibsen, Baron Ludwig Holberg, Alfred Jarry, Molière, and August Strindberg. He also published books on Aristophanes and Greek theater, the philosopher Aristotle and his *Poetics*, and on Shakespeare and his plays. He died in 1997.

❦ ❦ ❦

Henrik Ibsen was born on 20 March, 1828, in Skien, a small town to the south of Kristiania (now Oslo), the capital city of Norway, into a prosperous middle-class family. His mother, Marichen, took a lively interest in the arts, and Ibsen was introduced to the theatre at an early age. When he was six, however, his father's business failed, and Ibsen's childhood was spent in relative poverty, until he was forced to leave school and find employment as an apprentice pharmacist in Grimstad. In 1846, an affair with a housemaid ten years older than him produced an illegitimate son, whose upbringing Ibsen was compelled to pay for until the boy was in his teens, though he saw nothing of him. Ibsen's family relationships in general were not happy, and after the age of twenty-two, he never saw either of his parents again, and kept in touch with them only through his sister Hedvig's letters.

While still working as a pharmacist, Ibsen was studying for university, in pursuit of a vague ambition to become a doctor. He failed the entrance examination, however, and at the age of twenty, launched his literary career with the publication in 1850 of a verse play, *Catiline*, which sold a mere fifty copies, having already been rejected by the Danish Theatre in Kristiania. Drama in Norwegian was virtually non-existent at this time, and the low status of the language reflected Norway's own position, as a province of Denmark, for most of the preceding five centuries. Kristiania, the capital, was one of Europe's smallest, with fewer than 30,000 inhabitants, and communications were primitive.

A Play a Year

However, change, as far as the theatre was concerned, was already under way, and Ibsen and his younger contemporary [Bjørnstjerne] Bjørnson were among the prime movers. Another was the internationally famous violinist, Ole Bull, who founded a Norwegian-language theatre in his home town of Bergen, and invited Ibsen to become its first resident dramatist in 1851, with a commitment to write one play each year, to be premièred on January 2nd, the anniversary of the theatre's founding.

During his time at Bergen, Ibsen wrote five plays, mainly historical in content: *St. John's Night*, a comedy which he later disowned, loosely based on *A Midsummer Night's Dream*; *The Warrior's Barrow*, a reworking of a one-act verse play first staged in Kristiania; *Lady Inger of Østråt*, a five-act drama set in 16th-century Trondheim, on the theme of Norwegian independence; *The Feast at Solhaug*, which went on to be commercially published; and a romantic drama, *Olaf Liljekrans*, to complete his contractual obligations in Bergen.

Ibsen had meanwhile met his future wife, Suzannah Thoresen, and the offer of a post as artistic director of the newly-created Norwegian Theatre in Kristiania must have been very welcome. Ibsen took up his post in September 1857, and not the least of his responsibilities was to compete for audiences with the long-established Danish Theatre in Kristiania. A successful first season was accordingly crucial, and his own new play, *The Vikings at Helgeland*, set in 10th-century Norway, and based on material drawn from the Norse sagas, was an important contribution. By 1861, however, the Danish Theatre was clearly winning the battle, in part by extending its Norwegian repertoire, and Ibsen's theatre was forced to close, in the summer of 1862.

Now unemployed, Ibsen successfully applied for a government grant to collect folk-tales in the Norwegian hinterland. During this period he also wrote *Love's Comedy*, a verse play on the theme of modern marriage, and a five-act historical drama, *The Pretenders*, now re-

garded as his first major play, premièred at the Kristiania Theatre in January 1864, under Ibsen's own direction. A few months later, financed by another government grant, Ibsen left Norway for Copenhagen on
April 2nd, 1864, beginning a journey that would take
him on to Rome, and international recognition.

More Personal Themes
Brand, the first fruit of Ibsen's self-imposed exile, sees
him abandoning historical themes, and drawing on his
own experience more directly, basing his uncompro-
mising hero on a fanatical priest who had led a religious
revival in Ibsen's home town of Skien in the 1850's.
Like all of Ibsen's plays, *Brand* was published before it
was staged, in March 1866, and received its first full
performance almost twenty years later, in 1885 at the
Nya Theatre in Stockholm, though it seems clear that
like *Peer Gynt*, his next play, *Brand* was intended to be
read, rather than acted.

Ibsen wrote *Peer Gynt* at Rome, Ischia and Sorrento,
through the summer of 1867, using material from Asb-
jarnsen's recently-published *Norwegian Folk-Tales*, as
well as the darker corners of his own life, but the end
result is regarded as containing some of his finest dramatic writing, with the irrepressible Peer at the other
end of the moral spectrum from Brand, a typical example of Ibsen's fondness for opposites or antitheses in his
dramatic work.

The following spring, Ibsen left Rome for Berchtes-
gaden in the Bavarian Alps, to work on a new play, *The
League of Youth*, which was premièred at the Kristiania
Theatre in October 1869, and attracted some hostility
for its satirical portrayal of contemporary politicians. A
few weeks later, Ibsen travelled to Egypt, to represent
his country at the official opening of the Suez Canal.

On his return, Ibsen began work on what he regarded

as his greatest achievement, the mammoth ten-act *Emperor and Galilean*, dramatising the conflict between Christianity and paganism, through the life of Julian the Apostate. Published in Copenhagen in October 1873, to much critical acclaim, the play nonetheless had to wait over a century before it was staged in full, an eight-hour marathon in Oslo in 1987.

Ibsen Is Knighted

By this time, Ibsen's fame had brought him tempting offers to return to Norway, as well as recognition at the highest level in the form of a knighthood, of the Order of St Olaf. However, apart from a brief sojourn in Kristiania in the summer of 1874, he remained in Germany, moving from Dresden to Munich the following year, to commence writing *The Pillars of Society*, completed in 1877, the first in a series of 'social problem' plays, although its large cast requirements make it nowadays something of a theatrical rarity. By contrast, his next play, *A Doll's House*, has seldom been absent from the stage since its Copenhagen première in December 1879, and the challenge it offers to male hypocrisy and so-called 'family values' has ensured its continuing popularity.

In Ibsen's characteristic manner, *Ghosts* in effect reverses the situation of *A Doll's House*, showing the tragic consequences of a wife's failure to break free from a disastrous marriage. Its exposure of taboo subjects like venereal disease, however, still retains the power to shock, and it was at first rejected by all Ibsen's preferred theatres. After publication, almost two years elapsed before *Ghosts* was staged in Scandinavia, and the world première in fact took place in Chicago, in May 1882.

Ibsen was angered by his countrymen's reception of *Ghosts*, and *An Enemy of the People*, with its ill-concealed attack on the Norwegian establishment, is to an extent a vehicle for that anger, as well as for Ibsen's sceptical views on democracy. The play thus offended liberals and conservatives alike, but not enough to impede its staging, and it was premièred in Kristiania in January 1883, to mixed reviews.

The initial reaction to *The Wild Duck*, published in November of the following year, was largely one of bewilderment, although it was produced without delay in all the major Scandinavian venues. While the 'original sin' of the drama, the housemaid made pregnant by her master and married off to a convenient dupe, echoes that of *Ghosts*, Ibsen's use of symbolism appeared to sit uneasily with the naturalistic dialogue, and indeed still troubles modern audiences.

Controversy and Scandal

However, Ibsen was moving away from the concerns of the 'problem play' towards a more personal, oblique utterance, and the controversy which dogged his work scarcely lessened with the publication of *Rosmersholm*, in November 1886. Especially noteworthy for the creation of Rebecca West, one of Ibsen's most compelling characters, its witches' brew of ingredients even included incest, and it caused a minor scandal.

Ibsen's reputation was by now unassailable, however, and in Germany particularly, the innovative productions of the Saxe-Meiningen company had won him an eager following. In England, the enthusiasm of Edmund Gosse, and later William Archer, ensured that several of his plays were at least available in translation, but the first significant staging of his work in London had to wait until June 1889, with the Novelty Theatre production of *A Doll's House*.

Meanwhile, *The Lady From the Sea* fared well enough at the box office, with simultaneous premières in Kristiania and Weimar, on 12 February, 1889, though again

its complex amalgam of dreamy symbolism, evolution-
ary theory, and the daily routine of the Wangel household in northern Norway, tended to confuse audiences,
and is still something of an obstacle to production.

Hedda Gabler, premièred in Munich at the Residenz-
theater in January 1891, is now Ibsen's most popular
play, but attracted fierce criticism in its day, largely on
account of the character of Hedda herself. Arguably Ibsen's finest creation, Hedda's contempt for the sacred
roles of wife and mother seemed the more offensive in
that Ibsen provided no explanation for it, no inherited
moral taint, and she continues to unnerve us even today, like a glimpse into the abyss.

In that same year, 1891, there were no fewer than
five London productions of Ibsen plays, including
Hedda Gabler, and the publication of George Bernard
Shaw's seminal critique, *The Quintessence of Ibsenism*,
helped assure his place in the permanent English repertoire. Ibsen himself returned to Norway in July, a national hero, though he suffered the indignity of hearing
his achievement disparaged by the rising young novelist Knut Hamsun, at a public lecture in October.

May Sun in a September Life

In his declining years, Ibsen increasingly sought the
company of young female admirers, and his relationships with Emilie Bardach, Helene Raff, and finally
Hildur Andersen, find their way into his later plays, notably *The Master Builder*, in which Ibsen also returns to
the theme of self, which had inspired his early masterpieces, *Brand* and *Peer Gynt*. The burden of fame, the
generational conflict between age and youth, Ibsen's
personal concerns, are explored in the relationship between the successful middle-aged architect Solness and
the twenty-something 'free spirit' Hilde Wangel. Although the all-pervasive tower metaphor puzzled some

critics, given that [doctor and psychologist Sigmund] Freud had still to explain such things, the play was an instant success, going on from its première in Berlin in January 1893, to productions in Scandinavia, Paris, Chicago and London within the year. . . .

John Gabriel Borkman, published three years later, and premiéred in Helsinki in January 1897, achieves in prose the poetic grandeur of *Brand*. . . .

Ibsen was now permanently resident in Kristiania, venerated wherever he went, and his seventieth birthday, on 20 March, 1898, was the occasion for widespread rejoicing. His collected works were in preparation in both Denmark and Germany, and his international fame rivalled that of [Leo] Tolstoy. It is fitting, therefore, that Ibsen's last play, *When We Dead Awaken*, should have been premièred on 15 January, 1900, in effect launching the next century, at Kristiania's new National Theatre, the confident expression of that Norwegian identity which Ibsen and Bjørnson, whose statues graced its entrance, did so much to promote.

Finally, like almost all of Ibsen's plays, *When We Dead Awaken* is a response to the author's psychic needs, part confession, part exorcism, and it can be argued that the ageing sculptor Rubek's return to his first inspiration, Irene, now confined in a sanatorium, represents Ibsen's feelings of guilt over his neglect of his wife Suzannah, and his belated acknowledgement that she had been the real sustaining force behind his work. The tone of *When We Dead Awaken* is accordingly elegiac, an appropriate coda to Ibsen's long career. Two months later, in March 1900, he suffered the first of a series of strokes which was to lead to his death, in Kristiania, on 23 May, 1906.

Oscar Wilde: A Life of Wit and Woe

Thomas Siebold

The playwright Oscar Wilde is best known for his wit, which was shown in both his daily life and in his writings, and for the sexual scandal that destroyed the final years of his life. In the following selection, editor and author Thomas Siebold provides an overview of the experiences and relationships that shaped the Irish writer's life. Wilde struggled for years as a playwright before finally achieving success on the London stage with works such as *Lady Windermere's Fan* and his most popular play, *The Importance of Being Earnest*. Wilde's popularity dwindled in 1895 when he was convicted and sentenced to jail for two years on charges of gross indecency—Wilde had engaged in a homosexual relationship, which was illegal in England at the time. More than a century after Wilde's death, his plays continue to be performed on both stage and screen.

❧ ❧ ❧

Oscar Fingal O'Flahertie Wills Wilde was born in the family's Dublin home in 1854. When he was just one year old his father's increasing wealth allowed them

Thomas Siebold, "Oscar Wilde: A Biography," *Readings on* The Importance of Being Earnest, edited by Thomas Siebold. San Diego: Greenhaven Press, 2001. Copyright © 2001 by Greenhaven Press, Inc. Reproduced by permission.

to move into a large Georgian house, one of the finest in Dublin, and hire a maid, six servants, and a governess, who, along with Lady Wilde, tutored the children at home. . . .

At Trinity and Oxford

When Wilde was just seventeen, he won a scholarship to a notable Protestant university, Trinity College, in Dublin. Wilde distinguished himself at Trinity. He received several awards for his scholarship in the classics, including the prestigious Berkeley Gold Medal for Greek. He was greatly influenced by two far-reaching intellects: the Reverend J.P. Mahaffy and Robert Yelverton Tyrrell. Tyrrell was a quiet but talented professor of Latin while Mahaffy, the chair of the ancient history department, was an enormous intellect who often flaunted his scholarship. Unfortunately, Mahaffy and Wilde eventually clashed, and the playwright would later satirize the pretentious professor.

In 1872 Willie, Wilde's brother who also attended Trinity, traveled to London to study law. Wilde, twenty years old and anxious for new experiences, also left Trinity after winning a generous scholarship in classics at Oxford University. . . .

In 1876 Wilde began to write poetry in earnest, publishing numerous poems in Oxford and Irish periodicals. During his last year at Oxford, Wilde won the university prize for poetry for his poem "Ravenna," named after the city that he grew to love during his tour of Italy. Printed by the university as part of the prize, *Ravenna* was Wilde's first published book.

Despite his distinguished student years at college, the school administration surprisingly did not offer Wilde a teaching position. Wilde's future was unresolved: His father had died in April 1876; his mother, after her husband's death, had moved to London; and his brother Willie, who had given up his intention to be a lawyer, was practicing journalism in London. Hence, it was logical that Wilde would move there as well. Disappointed that he did not receive a teaching fellowship, Wilde went to London believing he was beginning a new life, but he was uncertain about the direction it would take. A close friend asked him what he wanted to accomplish there, and the young poet simply stated that he expected to be famous, and if not famous, he believed that he would be notorious.

Earning Fame in London

In London Wilde shared an apartment with an artist and old friend from Oxford, Frank Miles. Miles, a tall, good-looking man who had respectable artistic talent, maintained a studio in one of the rooms, where he was making a name for himself by drawing portraits of the most beautiful women in London. Through the invitations of these women, both Miles and Wilde attended very fashionable parties. Wilde's evening attire was outrageously flamboyant, characterized by velvet coats, bright ties, and silk stockings. It was not long before influential London socialites recognized Wilde as a desirable young aesthete who provided entertaining and meaningful insights into art and beauty. From Wilde's point of view, these early days in London were really part of his overall strategy to attain fame and notoriety.

In 1881, living on a meager income, he received a break with the production of *Patience*, a comic opera satirizing many British customs and traditions written by the famous team of W.S. Gilbert, librettist, and Arthur Sullivan, composer. The producer of the play hired Wilde to promote *Patience* by lecturing in America, which he did with style. Even at the U.S. customs station, Wilde's wit was evident when he stated that he had nothing to declare but his genius. Wilde was a great success in America, and crowds flocked to his lectures and treated him as a star. . . .

First Attempts as a Playwright

Wilde continued to write poetry throughout his first years after college, and early in 1881, after being turned down by several publishers, he published a collection of his poems at his own expense. Although he received some encouraging words from the accomplished poet Matthew Arnold, the critics were generally harsh. The cruelest blow came when his alma mater, Oxford, turned down his book of verse for its library.

Convinced that his ability to maintain brilliant and mesmerizing conversation was a skill that would help him write entertaining dramatic dialogue, Wilde turned his artistic attention to writing plays. His first drama, *Vera*, like his collection of poems, did not initially receive favorable attention. However, in 1881 the Adelphi Theatre in London agreed to produce the play. But just as the play was to begin rehearsals, the producer abruptly canceled it. *Vera* centers on events in Russia, and the untimely assassination of Czar Alexander II made the drama politically inappropriate since the czarina was the sister-in-law of England's Prince of Wales.

Wilde's second play, *The Duchess of Padua*, also met with failure. He began writing the play during his 1881 lecture tour of America. He wrote the play with the encouragement and support of a famous American actress, Mary Anderson. But when he finally finished the work in 1883 and sent a copy to her, she responded bluntly that she could not accept the play in its present form, explaining that the part did not fit her. It was not until 1891 that a New York theater staged *The Duchess of Padua* under a different name, *Guido Ferranti*. It failed after only three weeks.

Desperate for money, Wilde agreed in 1883 to a lecture tour of England, arranged by the organizers of his American circuit. Billed as "the Great Aesthete" Wilde's most popular lecture was entitled "Personal Impressions of America."

It was during this time that Wilde met and made friends with the famous painter James McNeill Whistler, himself a notorious wit. The friendship ended in bitterness, however, when the two began to verbally spar with one another. The final blow came when Whistler wrote a letter to the magazine *Truth*, in which he accused Wilde of plagiarizing his ideas. Wilde's rebuttal letter not only refuted Whistler's ideas but also ridiculed the artist's well-known egotism:

> Mr. James Whistler has had the impertinence to attack me with both venom and vulgarity in your columns. I hope you will allow me to state that the assertions contained in his letter are as deliberately untrue as they are deliberately offensive. . . . The only thoroughly original ideas I have ever heard him express have had reference to his own superiority over painters greater than himself. It is a trouble for any gentleman to have to notice the lucubrations [laborious studies] of so ill-bred and ignorant a person as Mr. Whistler.

Wilde's attack resulted in a hostile estrangement between the two men.

The energy spent fighting Whistler, combined with the loneliness of a burdensome lecture tour that eventually caused him to feel like an out-of-place curiosity, made Wilde return to London to recommit himself to writing. The only positive that emerged during the unsettling year of 1883 was Wilde's engagement to Constance Lloyd, a young woman whom he had met two years earlier through a family friend.

Wife and Children
On May 29, 1884, Wilde married Lloyd. She was a pretty and talented woman who attended art school,

sang, and liked to read. In short, she shared Wilde's interests. In a letter to a friend, Wilde describes his bride-to-be:

> I am going to be married to a beautiful girl called Constance Lloyd, a grave, slight, violet-eyed little Artemis, with great coils of heavy brown hair which make her flower-like head droop like a blossom, and wonderful ivory hands which draw music from the piano so sweet that the birds stop singing to listen to her.

Constance's guardians, her grandparents, left her a small inheritance that supported the couple as Wilde struggled to establish himself as a writer. In the early years of their marriage, Constance was supportive of Wilde's work, often showing up at his lectures wearing unorthodox costumes that reflected her husband's eccentric taste in clothing.

They had two sons: the first, Cyril, was born on June 5, 1885, and the second, Vyvyan, was born on November 5, 1886. Wilde's two sons were a source of joy for him. . . .

Establishing Himself as a Playwright

After more than a decade since writing *Vera*, Wilde constructed another play, *Lady Windermere's Fan*. In February 1892 this drama, which Wilde described as a modern drawing-room play, opened in London at the fashionable St. James Theatre, staged by the well-known actor and producer George Alexander. This debut of *Lady Windermere's Fan* initiated a remarkable three-year run for the playwright. A string of five successful plays made Wilde the rightful star of the London drama scene.

Lady Windermere's Fan focuses on a woman who sacrifices herself for her daughter. The play resonated well with audience members, and at the close of the opening performance, they gave the play and its author a standing ovation. Wilde stepped from behind the curtain, smoking a cigarette, and elegantly thanked the stylish audience by saying, "Ladies and Gentlemen. I have enjoyed this evening immensely. The actors have given us a charming rendering of a delightful play, and your appreciation has been most intelligent. I congratulate you on the great success of your performance, which persuades me that

Born in Dublin in 1854, Oscar Wilde became famous for his sophisticated, witty plays as well as his eccentricity in dress, tastes, and manners.

you think almost as highly of the play as I do."

Later the same year, Wilde's *Salome*, which he wrote in Paris in 1891, was scheduled to have its London debut at the Palace Theatre starring the beautiful Sarah Bernhardt. After weeks of rehearsal, the cast learned that the play, based on biblical stories, had not received a performance license. All plays in London were required to pass a censorship review according to the Theatres Act of 1843. Works scheduled for public performance had to receive a stamp of approval from the examiner of plays, Lord Chamberlain, and, if necessary, they would be altered to protect the decorum and well-being of the public. *Salome*, which had been staged earlier in Paris, seemed to Lord Chamberlain to be beyond repair, and the controversial play was denied a London performance. It was not until 1894 that *Salome* was translated from its original French into English and was published.

Despite the setback of *Salome*, Wilde soon scored another dramatic victory with *A Woman of No Importance*, produced by Beerbohm Tree at the Haymarket Theatre in April 1893. After spending nearly a month in 1892 at a health spa in Germany to recoup his energy, Wilde returned to England to finish writing the social comedy. The play received an enthusiastic reception from audiences and a generally favorable response from critics. The reviewers found fault with its technical aspects, but they had to admit that they loved watching it. Again Wilde displayed his adept use of language, his indefatigable wit, and his keen understanding of human nature and society. Although the play provided adequate financial resources for Wilde, it did not run as long as *Lady Windermere's Fan*.

In January 1895 Wilde's successful run continued with the opening of *An Ideal Husband* at the Haymarket Theatre. The twists of plot, intrigue, and blackmail in this play delighted the public. It enjoyed an immensely popular run of 111 performances, but it was discontinued when Wilde's name was sullied with a notorious libel case, a situation stemming from a very public accusation that he was having an illegal homosexual affair with the son of a well-known London figure. As with his other successful plays, audiences loved it and critics begrudgingly accepted it. The respectable playwright George Bernard Shaw, writing for the *Saturday Review*, reflected the typical critical opinion when he wrote that the play tricked the audience into frivolity, cleverly getting them to laugh angrily at his epigrams.

The Importance of Being Earnest

During the late summer and fall of 1894 Wilde retreated with his family to the seaside town of Worthing, Sussex, to write his most popular play, *The Importance of Being Earnest*. After just three weeks Wilde was confident that he had a play worthy of staging. In a letter to his friend Lord Alfred Douglas, Wilde exclaimed, "I have been doing nothing here but bathing and playwriting. My play is really very funny: I am quite delighted with it. But it is not shaped yet." Wilde sent his completed comedy to the influential producer George Alexander for review, writing in his cover letter, "It is called *Lady Lancing* on the cover: but the real title is *The Importance of Being Earnest*. When you read the play, you will see the punning title's meaning." Alexander rejected it but suggested it would play better if Wilde cut it from four acts to three. Wilde reworked the play in three acts, removing a lengthy scene concerning debt collection. At the time, bailiffs who wanted money for his outstanding debts were pursuing the playwright.

Fortunately for Wilde, the play that Alexander was staging at his popular St. James Theatre failed miserably and the producer closed it abruptly. After a number of alterations, Alexander agreed to stage Wilde's revised comedy, and after rushed and often frantic rehearsals, it opened a month later on February 14, 1895, with Alexander playing Jack Worthing. In a pre–opening night newspaper interview, a reporter asked the playwright if the play would be a success, to which Wilde deftly responded, "My dear fellow, you have got it all wrong. The play *is* a success. The only question is whether the first night's audience will be one." Despite terrible winter weather and one postponed opening night due to illness, the initial performance drew a full house. The play was a sensation; the audience rose to its feet at its conclusion and cheered wildly. The actor who played Algernon Moncrieff later stated that, in fifty-three years of acting, he had never seen such an overwhelmingly triumphant opening performance.

The critics of 1895 generally wrote favorable reviews of *Earnest*. One reviewer captured the reaction of the audience when he wrote, "It is delightful to see, it sends wave after wave of laughter curling and foaming round the theatre." However, the drama also drew criticism. Some reviewers felt that the play relied far too heavily on verbal pyrotechnics and that the wit frequently went annoyingly overboard. Others complained that the play lacked meaning and that Wilde's style was affected and contrived. Again, George Bernard Shaw led the charge:

> It amused me, of course; but unless comedy touches me as well as amuses me, it leaves me with a sense of having wasted my evening. I go to the theatre to be moved to laughter, not to be tickled or bustled into it; and this is why, though I laugh as much as anybody at a farcical comedy, I am out of spirits before the end of the second act, and out of temper before the end of the third.

Still others felt uncomfortable with the characters, claiming they were nothing more than vague vehicles to spout clever epigrams.

The play had run for a full month, enjoying full houses for each performance, when, on April 5, 1895, authorities arrested Oscar Wilde. His arrest and subsequent trial caused Alexander, acquiescing to societal prudery, to remove the playwright's name from the playbill and all advertising. *The Importance of Being Earnest* continued for one more month, but to smaller audiences. It ran for a total of eighty-one performances before Alexander shut it down, resulting in a loss of revenues. Today, of course, playgoers consider Wilde's farce to be one of the funniest ever written. Audiences around the world find something in the play that resonates with their experiences in society.

In 1886, at age thirty-two, Wilde met Robert Ross, the seventeen-year-old grandson of the governor general of Canada, and the two became lovers and friends for life. Whether Wilde's liaisons with Ross were his first homosexual experiences is hard to tell since many of his closest friends at Oxford and throughout his early adulthood were homosexuals. Nevertheless, Wilde's predilection for young men would be the vehicle for the tragedy of his life: his downfall and ultimate two-year imprisonment as a sodomite.

In England at that time it was illegal to practice homosexuality. Perhaps it is more accurate to say that one could be found guilty of homosexuality if one did not keep one's private life to oneself. Wilde, however, made his sexuality, like so many other aspects of his life, a matter of public record. The homosexual relationship that finally destroyed Wilde was with Lord Alfred Douglas, the third son of the eighth marquess of Queensberry. Wilde met Douglas, sixteen years Wilde's junior, in 1891 while Wilde was visiting his former college, Magdalen, where Douglas was enrolled as a student. Wilde fell desperately in love with this young man, who was known for his good looks and his poetic ability. Douglas, nicknamed Bosie, returned Wilde's affection, and the two, despite many bitter quarrels and spats, became lovers. In a letter to his friend and former lover, Robert Ross, Wilde exclaims his passion for the young Bosie:

> My Dearest Bobbie, Bosie has insisted on stopping here for sandwiches. He is quite like a narcissus—so white and gold. I will come either Wednesday or Thursday night to your rooms. Send me a line. Bosie is so tired: he lies like a hyacinth on the sofa, and I worship him.
>
> You dear boy. Ever yours, Oscar.

The two spent much of their time together, and Wilde spent vast amounts of money entertaining the young man, often pushing his personal finances to the brink of ruin.

Douglas's father, a rather abrupt, mean-spirited man who no longer lived with his wife and son, heard of the Wilde relationship and demanded that Douglas break it off. Lord Queensberry was known as a forceful man who had made a reputation in the world of boxing as a successful promoter and initiator of a set of boxing regulations called the Queensberry rules. At one point Lord Queensberry told his son directly that his "intimacy with this man Wilde must either cease or I will disown you." In response, Douglas wired his father with the terse message, "What a funny little man you are." The elder Douglas, enraged, increased his demands to the point of threatening both his son and Wilde with physical violence. In an effort to confront Wilde, Lord Queensberry left a visiting card at Wilde's mens' club in which he directly accused Wilde of posing as a sodomite. Shocked at Lord Queensberry's breach of etiquette and perhaps frightened, Wilde wrote a prophetic letter to Robert Ross: "Since I last saw you something has happened—Bosie's father has left a card at my Club with hideous words on it. I don't see anything now but a criminal prosecution—my whole life seems ruined by this man." At one point Lord Queensberry's rage boiled to such a point that he and a prizefighter escort showed up at the 1895 opening night performance of *The Importance of Being Earnest*, intending to disrupt the play by shouting insults and throwing rotten vegetables on stage. Fortunately, the police stopped him at the door.

Wilde on Trial

Encouraged by Douglas, who wanted desperately to see his father humiliated, Wilde hired solicitor Sir Edward Clarke to prosecute Lord Queensberry for libel. Clarke had a solid reputation for taking cases in which he was sure that his client was innocent. When Clarke asked Wilde if Queensberry's charges were true, Wilde responded by saying unequivocally that they were not. Perhaps if Wilde had answered honestly, Clarke would have dropped the case and helped Wilde avoid the tragedy that was about to unfold.

Unfortunately for Wilde, his homosexual activities were well known by a rather substantial group of people in London. In fact, several very damaging letters written by Wilde to his lover were in the hands of potential blackmailers. It turns out that Douglas had given one of his suits to a young man he had been seeing, not realizing that Wilde's letters were still in the pocket. The momentum turned against Wilde. Queensberry hired a brilliant barrister, Edward Carson, who, ironically, had been a friend and classmate of Wilde's at Trinity College. Carson quickly aligned numerous witnesses to attest to Wilde's homosexual behavior.

At the time, Wilde received conflicting advice. Many of his friends, realizing that Wilde was facing a serious situation that he would probably lose, told him to drop the charges and let the situation cool down by leaving the country for a while. Contrarily, Alfred Douglas, blinded by his own self-centeredness and motivated by a consuming drive to hurt his father, urged Wilde to continue with the libel case.

In the witness box, Wilde was his usual brilliant self, answering questions with wit and aplomb. But the evidence was stacked against him, and it quickly became apparent that Wilde's charge of libel was unfounded because the playwright was indeed a homosexual. After three days of trial, Clarke withdrew as counsel and Wilde lost his case. Queensberry now felt justified, and he went on the offensive by obtaining a warrant for Wilde's arrest. Despite the impending calamity, Wilde had an opportunity to take a train to France and thereby avoid the arrest warrant, but he refused. With the urging of his lawyer, Douglas fled to Europe just before the start of Wilde's trial.

Wilde stood alone facing twenty-five charges of gross indecency according to the Criminal Law Amendment Act of 1885, which allowed the courts to imprison someone for homosexual acts. From the stand Wilde denied all charges of indecency, claiming that he was fascinated by youth but that he had done nothing indecent. On May 1, 1895, the jury could not agree on a verdict, so the judge scheduled a second trial to begin on May 20. The public was both shocked and fascinated as the details of the two trials were reported in the newspapers, bringing homosexuality into the public domain for the first time.

The jury found Wilde guilty, and the judge sentenced him to two years of hard labor at the harsh Reading Gaol prison. Wilde later described his first days of incarceration to his friend Frank Harris:

> The cell was appalling: I could hardly breathe in it, and the food turned my stomach; the smell and sight of it were enough: I did not eat anything for days and days and days, I could not even swallow the bread;

and the rest of the food was uneatable; I lay on the so-called bed and shivered all night long. . . . After some days I got so hungry I had to eat a little, nibble at the outside of the bread, and drink some of the liquid; whether it was tea, coffee or gruel, I could not tell. As soon as I really ate anything it produced violent diarrhea and I was ill all day and all night. From the beginning I could not sleep, I grew weak and had wild delusions. . . . The hunger made you weak; but the inhumanity was the worst of it. What devilish creatures men are. I had never known anything about them. I had never dreamt of such cruelties.

During his two years of hard labor, Wilde suffered immensely: He lost his health, he anguished mentally and psychologically, he was divorced, he went bankrupt, and he lost his esteem in the eye of the public. The absence of common everyday amenities were the hardest to bear for the playwright: conversation, books, and writing paper. His name was so loathed that his wife and children, traveling in Switzerland under a false name, were required to leave a hotel when it became known who they were. . . .

His Final Years
Upon his release from prison, Wilde's longtime friend Robert Ross helped the frail playwright get resettled. Wilde assumed the name Sebastian Melmoth and moved to Dieppe, France, never to return to England again. The name of Melmoth was based on a character from a play, *Melmoth the Wanderer*, written by Wilde's great uncle Charles Robert Maturin. Eventually Wilde's strength returned enough that he began to write poetry again, creating his last serious work, *The Ballad of Reading Gaol*. This ballad explores the pain of prisoners as they suffer the last days with a condemned inmate, a soldier who killed his wife. Although the poem did not rejuvenate Wilde's literary career when he was alive, it is

considered posthumously as one of his most movingly written poems.

Despite his bitterness toward Lord Alfred Douglas and the fact that Constance had threatened to cut off his financial support if he ever saw Douglas again, Wilde gave in to Douglas's persistent requests and agreed to see his former lover. Unable to overcome his counterproductive passion for Douglas, Wilde seemingly reconciled with the younger man and they traveled throughout Italy together. Outraged, Constance refused to see Wilde herself or to allow him to visit their sons.

Then, in April 1898, Wilde learned that Constance, age forty, had died of complications from a spinal operation. Wilde was overwhelmed by the unexpected news of her death: "It is awful. I don't know what to do. If we had only met once and kissed each other. It is too late. How awful life is." Wilde visited her grave and was hurt that her family had chosen to omit Wilde from her name on the tombstone:

> It was very tragic seeing her name carved on a tomb, her surname—my name not mentioned of course— just "Constance Mary, daughter of Horace Lloyd, Q.C." and a verse from Revelations. I bought some flowers. I was deeply affected, with a sense, also, of the uselessness of all regrets. Nothing could have been otherwise, and life is a very terrible thing.

For the rest of the year Wilde wandered around France, Italy, and Switzerland, sometimes with Douglas, sometimes with Ross, and often alone.

Eventually Wilde settled into an apartment at the inexpensive Hotel d'Alsace in Paris. Living off the modest money left to him by Constance, Wilde was pressed financially. Many of his former friends neglected him financially, including Douglas, whom Wilde had earlier showered with gifts and money.

In the middle months of 1900 Wilde suffered progressively severe headaches. An attending doctor hastily recommended an ear operation that left Wilde in great pain and in need of a full-time attendant. Cognizant that he might be dying, Wilde telegraphed his faithful friend Robert Ross, requesting that he come immediately, writing, "Terribly weak. Please come." Poor and dying, Wilde quipped from his deathbed, "I am dying beyond my means. I will never outlive the century. The English people would not stand for it." On November 30, 1900, Wilde died comforted by Ross and a few other friends. Just before his death, Wilde received his last rites after becoming a deathbed convert to the Roman Catholic Church.

Anton Chekhov: Man of Letters and Medicine

Avrahm Yarmolinsky

Anton Chekhov (1860–1904), the son of a Russian serf, emerged from modest beginnings to become a successful playwright and medical doctor. He worked tirelessly throughout his life, earning his living as a physician so that he might steal time for his less lucrative career—writing. Chekhov's stories, often set in the Russian countryside, portray the dreariness of Russian life but also the playwright's love of nature. He experienced a few failed productions before his plays *Uncle Vanya*, *The Three Sisters*, and *The Cherry Orchard* met with enthusiastic receptions.

Ironically, the compassionate doctor who often treated the downtrodden at no cost ignored his own frail health much of his life. Concerned with civic duty, he traveled in 1890 to the penal colonies of Sakhalin Island in Siberia, where he took a census of the population and recorded the degrading conditions. He subsequently published a treatise on his findings.

Avrahm Yarmolinsky recounts Chekhov's struggles and triumphs in his introduction to *The Portable Chekhov*. Yarmolinsky was one of the foremost modern authorities and translators of Russian literature and the author of

Avrahm Yarmolinsky, "Introduction," *The Portable Chekhov*, by Anton Chekhov, edited by Avrahm Yarmolinksy. New York: Viking Press, 1947. Copyright © 1947 by Viking Penguin, Inc., renewed in 1975 by Avrahm Yarmolinsky. Reproduced by permission of Viking Penguin, a division of Penguin Group (USA) Inc.

works on Ivan Turgenev and Fyodor Dostoyevsky. Russian born, he came to the United States in 1913 and was married to poet Babette Deutsch.

❦   ❦   ❦

Though generally reticent about his personal history, Chekhov never attempted to conceal the sordidness of his beginnings. On one occasion he gave a fairly clear hint at what his early environment had been. As a successful young writer he made this suggestion to a fellow author: "Write a story of how a young man, the son of a serf, a former grocery boy, chorister, high school lad and university student, who was brought up to respect rank, to kiss priests' hands, to revere other people's ideas, to give thanks for every morsel of bread, who was whipped many times, who without rubbers traipsed from pupil to pupil, who used his fists and tormented animals, who was fond of dining with rich relatives, who was hypocritical in his dealings with God and men gratuitously, out of the mere consciousness of his insignificance—write how this youth squeezes the slave out of himself drop by drop, and how, waking up one fine morning, he feels that in his veins flows no longer the blood of a slave but that of a real man. . . ." He was talking about himself. . . .

Chekhov was indeed the son of a serf and would have been born one himself, had not his grandfather, an acquisitive peasant, managed to purchase the family's freedom. His father rose in the world, becoming the owner of a grocery, or rather of a general store, which also dispensed liquor. This was in the wretched little southern seaport of Taganrog, where Anton was born on January 17, 1860, the third child in a family that was to include five boys and a girl.

The grocer was a strict disciplinarian who administered beatings to his children as a parental duty and forced them to attend church services, of which he was himself passionately fond. . . .

The population of Taganrog included a great many Greeks, some of them wealthy importers. They maintained a one-room parish school of their own for the children of the poor, which was presided over by an ignorant and brutal master. Anton was sent there in the hope that he might eventually obtain the position of bookkeeper with one of the Greek merchants. After a year's attendance, during which he didn't learn as much as the Greek alphabet, he was transferred, at the age of nine, to the local *gimnaziya*, a combined grammar and high school. There he gave a poor account of himself, partly perhaps because he had little time for study. Among other things, he had to play watchdog for his father at the store, where he became familiar with all the tricks of short-weighting and short-changing.

Anton was sixteen when the store failed and his father escaped debtors' prison by absconding. He went to Moscow, where his two older sons were studying. The rest of the family soon followed, except Anton. Left to shift for himself, he continued at school, earning his way by tutoring and getting some help from relatives. His situation was not a happy one, but at least his natural gaiety was no longer restrained by an oppressive domestic atmosphere.

The Pursuit of Medicine

After graduating from high school, he joined the family and, having a small stipend from the Taganrog municipality, entered the university as a medical student. The Chekhovs were in a sad way. Anton became virtually the head of the house, and it was to him that the family looked for support, as it was to go on doing through the years. That winter, the story goes, in order to buy a pie for his mother's birthday, he wrote a piece for a comic weekly. That brought him his first literary earnings.

"Oh, with what trash I began," Chekhov once said, "my God, with what trash!" He supplied the humbler public prints with fillers of all sorts: jokes, legends for cartoons, advertisements, aphorisms, recipes, all in a comic vein. He wrote sketches, theatrical notices, and short short stories. He even produced, on a bet, a romantic tale purporting to be a translation, and a full-length thriller, in which a *femme fatale* is murdered under baffling circumstances. (Unlike so many of his early pieces, this novel was not allowed to lie decently buried in the files of the paper in which it first appeared, but sixty years later was seized upon by the ghouls of Hollywood.) He also tried his hand at journalism. This was not yet serious writing, but it meant being occupied with serious subject matter. He was turning out a great amount of copy, being able to scribble under any conditions, whenever and wherever he pleased, and sometimes dashing off a sketch—such as "The Siren"—without a single erasure. The stuff wrote itself. . . .

On receiving his medical diploma, he was for a while in charge of a hospital in a small town. Even earlier he had begun accumulating the knowledge of the peasant patients and provincial doctors who figure in his stories. After a few months he returned to Moscow to hang out his shingle. He was a hard-working and conscientious physician, but medicine did not prove his salvation, certainly not in a financial sense. His patients were mostly poor people, and in any case he regarded healing the sick as a humane duty, scarcely a means of livelihood. He continued to rely chiefly on his pen for his earnings and although he went on writing at a great rate, only the worst of the worrying and pinching was over. . . .

His Literary Talent Surfaces

Meanwhile there began to turn up among his writings, and with increasing frequency, pieces that gave promise of the harvest to come: bits of pure comedy, sharp character sketches, little masterpieces of pathos, candid studies of the folly of the heart. He was maturing, slowly, unevenly, yet unmistakably. To his astonishment he was discovering that he had a public and that, indeed, he was the object of critical consideration, in spite of the fact that he had not yet made the dignified "stout" monthlies. When, early in 1886, he scraped together enough rubles to take him to Petersburg, the intellectual and publishing center of the country, he was received "like the Shah of Persia." And then came a marvelous letter from [Russian novelist Dmitry] Grigorovich, one of the Olympians, telling him that he was the foremost of the younger writers and pleading with him to take his talent seriously. Toward the end of the year when he again visited the capital he found that he was "the most fashionable writer" there. In the interim he had brought out a second and successful book of stories (the first had passed unnoticed), and had begun to write for the great daily, *Novoye vremya* (New Time), which meant better rates and greater prestige.

He was developing a literary conscience. Formerly, he joked, writing had been like eating pancakes; now when he took up his pen he trembled. He was anxious to undertake something serious, something that would engage all his powers and that he could work at without haste. In the summer of 1887 he fulfilled at least the first of these wishes by writing a drama, which he called *Ivanov* after its unhappy hero. He had always loved the theater and had written plays even as a schoolboy. *Ivanov*, however, was a failure, which he was in haste to forget, and he was soon at work on his first serious long narrative, "The Steppe." For this leisurely, tender, evocative "history of a journey" he drew largely upon childhood memories of the great southern plain. But the vein of comedy was not to dry up all at once. In a few days he dashed off *The Boor*, which he described as "an empty Frenchified little vaudeville piece." It proved to be a box-office hit that was to entertain generations of Russians. He was to write several more such skits, most of them dramatizations of his own early stories, but henceforth the comic spirit was practically absent from his fiction.

To his surprise, as much as to his delight, in the autumn of 1888 he received the [Russian] Academy's Pushkin Prize for distinguished literary achievement. . . .

The Social Evils of Sakhalin

Without being political-minded, Chekhov was yet fully aware of social evils and had a strong sense of civic responsibility. Here too he felt that what counted was individual initiative, personal effort. This attitude makes intelligible a somewhat puzzling episode in his life. In the spring of 1890 he abandoned his manuscripts and his practice, his family and his friends, and traveled six thousand miles by train, by boat, by sledge, by coach, under the most exhausting and sometimes dangerous conditions—his was before the construction of the Trans-Siberian Railroad—to reach the penal colony on the island of Sakhalin. He spent over three months there, visiting practically every settlement—in fact, he claimed that single-handed he took a census of the population—and returned home via the Indian Ocean with material for a book. This was published between boards five years later. It is a hodge-podge of statistics, anecdotes, detailed geographical and historical data, thumbnail portraits, hardly redeemed by some pages that rival [novelist Fyodor] Dostoevsky's *Memoirs from the Dead House* in the candor with which they depict the degradation to which man can be reduced. Chekhov was glad to have written the book and proud to think of "this coarse convict's garb" hanging in his literary wardrobe. But was it for this satisfaction that he had endured the hardships of the trip to and of the sojourn on Sakhalin? . . .

He made other attempts in that direction. Early in 1892 he traveled into the famine-stricken provinces to organize relief, and was nearly lost in a blizzard. Later in the year, when central Russia was threatened with cholera, he acted as medical supervisor of the district in which he was living. With characteristic candor he confessed to a friend that he was in the vexing position of being able to read of nothing but cholera, to think of nothing but diarrhoea, while feeling indifferent to the people he was treating. It was equally characteristic that he should give up every other activity for an entire summer in order to help them. He took an active part in the building of village schools near his home and interested himself in a project of founding a settlement house in Moscow. In 1897 he was a volunteer censustaker, going from one log cabin to another, in spite of illness.

A Retreat to Melihovo

Two years after his return from Sakhalin Chekhov settled in the country. Since his student days he had summered there, for much as he loved the bustle and the human contacts of the city, he relished the solitude and serenity that the rural scene offered. Now he bought an estate of six hundred acres near the village of Melihovo, in the province of Moscow, and made a home there for his parents, his sister, and his younger brothers. One reason why he wished to leave town was that his health was poor. He said he was like an old cupboard coming apart. . . .

Even at its best, the place could not hold him. The master of Melihovo was a restless man, craving new impressions, eager for all that was strange and fresh. He made frequent trips to Moscow, where he was profusely fêted. He visited friends in the provinces, sailed up and down the Volga, traveled to the Crimea and the Caucasus, and in Suvorin's company saw France and Italy. European comforts, European culture made Russia seem more drab and dingy than ever. His return from Sakhalin by the Orient route had whetted his appetite for the exotic. He longed to go to South America. He wanted to see Chicago. Lack of funds and lack of courage, according to him, prevented him from realizing these dreams. Probably lack of health also had a good deal to do with it.

On one of his trips to Moscow he was dining in a restaurant with Suvorin when he had a severe hemorrhage of the lungs. With his usual nonchalance, he went about his business as soon as the bleeding stopped, only to suffer a relapse three days later. He was taken to a hospital. This was in March 1897. An examination—the first he had permitted—showed that he was far gone in consumption. . . .

Doctors' Orders

The doctors prescribed a strict regimen, country air, and residence in a southern climate, and they forbade him to practice medicine. He was not the man to take their orders seriously. But that autumn he did go abroad for his health. He settled in Nice, and in the spring went up to Paris. . . .

He could not stay abroad indefinitely. Whatever interest the foreign scene had for him, and that interest paled since he was ill, the pull of home was a strong one. On his return he was forced to give up Melihovo and go to live in Yalta, in the mild air of the southern coast of the Crimea.

He had visited the resort once or twice before, and it had depressed him profoundly. Now he was condemned to live in the Godforsaken place, where, he said, even the bacilli were asleep. It was exile to a warm Siberia, a balmy Devil's Island. . . .

The exile did not do for him what it should have. He did not get the proper diet or nursing, and he kept breaking away to take trips that cannot have benefited his health. His condition grew steadily worse. Nevertheless he was able to write. Such memorable stories as "The Man in a Shell," "Gooseberries," "The Darling," "On Official Business," "The Lady with the Pet Dog," were composed during those years. He also prepared his collected works for the press—not an unmixed pleasure, since he was dissatisfied with much that he had written and disgusted with his early stuff. They were issued in ten volumes in 1899—1901 under the imprint of A.F. Marx. He had sold his works to that publisher for 75,000 rubles, becoming, as he said, "a Marxist for life."

False Starts at Playwriting

It was during these years that Chekhov composed his better known plays. He had made a fiasco of his first attempt at playwriting with *Ivanov*, which was written and staged in Moscow in 1887. Two years later he rewrote the play for a revival in Petersburg and found the work of revision excruciating. He decided that he was no playwright. "Shoot me," he wrote to a friend, "if I go mad and occupy myself with what is not my business." In its revised form *Ivanov* proved a success, but his next piece, *The Wood Demon*, put on the same year, fell flat, and he disliked it so much that he refused to have it published. It was six years before he tried his hand at playwriting again. *The Sea Gull* was produced in Petersburg in 1896. Its failure verged on a scandal. The unhappy author swore that he would never attempt a play again. Yet in 1898 his *Uncle Vanya*, a revised version of *The Wood Demon*, was produced in the provinces and met with a favorable reception. At the close of the same year a newly formed company which went by the name of The Moscow Art Theatre performed *The Sea Gull* with great success. This was the beginning of the association between Chekhov and the Art Theatre, which persisted in spite of the fact that he was not wholly satisfied with the way in which his plays were interpreted. All of them, including the last two: *The Three Sisters* and *The Cherry Orchard*, became the very backbone of the repertory of the Art Theatre, which, in fact, adopted the gull as its emblem.

The role of Irina in *The Sea Gull* was played by Olga Knipper. Chekhov met the actress at a rehearsal. Within less than three years, on May 25, 1901, they were married. He was then forty-one and his bride thirty-one. . . .

The year before his marriage Chekhov was elected honorary member of the newly created Section of Belles Lettres in the National Academy of Sciences. He was at this time the most outstanding literary figure in Russia, next to Tolstoy. He did not long wear the academic laurels, however. In 1902 Maxim Gorky was accorded the same honor, but as he was then under indictment for a political offense, the authorities succeeded in having the election annulled. Thereupon Chekhov resigned from the august body. Though his protest was not a public one, the gesture was significant for a man of his temper. He had long since abandoned any attachment to the ideas that Suvorin championed in his paper. For at least a decade Chekhov's public—and that meant all literate Russia—had been taking it for granted that he belonged in the liberal camp. He still had no patience with cut-and-dried ideologies, owed no allegiance to any political group, nor did he show any leanings toward socialism. On occasion he could bracket "sulky-faced Marxists" with police inspectors. But he was now definitely with those who looked forward to the speedy downfall of the autocratic regime. What cropped up in the writings of his last years was something above and beyond millennial hopes: a dissatisfaction with quietism, a welcoming of the violent change that he saw on the way. At twenty-eight he had asserted that there would never be a revolution in Russia. At forty he believed differently. The country, he felt, was emerging from its torpor and beginning, as he put it, "to hum like a beehive." He wanted to catch this new mood of wakening energies. Indeed, in his last story, "Betrothed," a girl breaks away from her confining home environment and goes out into the world, and it has been stated that in the first draft Nadya, the heroine, joins the revolutionists. Chekhov also spoke of wanting to write "a buoyant play." He did not write it. His last play, *The Cherry Orchard*, first staged the year before the upheaval of 1905, tolled the knell of old Russia rather than rang in the new. Nor did he witness its aborted start.

A Constrained Celebration

What with his trips north and the excitement attendant upon the production of his plays, his mode of living was scarcely what the doctor ordered. After he was married, he grew rapidly worse. The first night of *The Cherry Orchard* was set for January 17, 1904, the playwright's forty-fourth birthday. His friends turned the evening into a celebration of the twenty-fifth anniversary of his literary activity, although he had actually broken into print in 1880, twenty-four years previously. Shaken with coughing, Chekhov was hardly able to stand up to receive the ovation and listen to the addresses. He was critically ill that spring and yet, with the war against Japan in progress, he talked of going to the front as an army doctor. In June he was rushed to a health resort in the Black Forest and there, on July 2, he died. His body was taken to Moscow in a refrigerating car for the transportation of oysters. The last trick that Fate played on him was of the sort that it would have amused him to jot down in his notebook.

Toward the end of his life Chekhov remarked to a friend that people would stop reading him a year after his death. As a matter of fact, his vogue kept growing steadily until the cataclysm of 1917 and his position as the major figure of the Silver Age of Russian literature was becoming increasingly secure. During the harsh, strenuous revolutionary years his reputation suffered a partial eclipse, but by now it has regained its former luster, and his work is valued not alone for its intrinsic quality but also for the light that it throws on a dead past. Just when his compatriots, coping with the tasks and hardships of the new order, were looking away from Chekhov, the western world, especially England and America, was enthusiastically exploring him as a remarkable discovery. Indeed, shortly after the First World War, the homage paid to him in certain literary circles verged on a cult. That first fine careless rapture has since died down, and something closer to a just estimate of his significance can be arrived at.

Samuel Beckett: The Irish Experimentalist

David Pattie

Irishman Samuel Beckett (1906–1989) went from struggling writer of novels, short stories, and unpublished dramas to overnight success when his experimental play *Waiting for Godot* was produced in London in 1953. The drama, with only a handful of characters, a minimalist set, a questionable plot, and a debatable meaning, was a hit with audiences. *Waiting for Godot*, the story of two hoboes waiting for someone who never comes, is considered the benchmark in what became labeled the Theatre of the Absurd.

Author David Pattie describes the playwright's life, providing insight into his studies, the teaching posts that made him uneasy, his plight during World War II, his various literary pursuits, and the bouts with anxiety that plagued him on and off throughout his life. In Beckett's later years, he continued producing uniquely and visually fascinating plays, such as *Krapp's Last Tape* and *Endgame*, but *Waiting for Godot* is still the work for which he is best known.

Pattie is a senior lecturer in the performing arts department at the University College Chester in the United Kingdom, where he also heads the master of arts program. He has published chapters and articles on Beckett, modern

David Pattie, *The Complete Critical Guide to Samuel Beckett*. London: Routledge, 2000. Copyright © 2000 by David Pattie. All rights reserved. Reproduced by permission of the publisher.

British drama, Scottish theater, performance theory, and popular performance styles and has reviewed books for theater publications.

❧ ❧ ❧

Samuel Barclay Beckett was born on Good Friday, April 13th, 1906, in Cooldrinagh, the Beckett family home in Foxrock, County Dublin. He was the youngest child: a brother, Frank, had been born almost four years earlier, on the 26th of July 1902. Beckett was born into a reasonably wealthy family. His father, William Beckett (more commonly known as Bill) worked as a quantity surveyor in Dublin; the business was successful enough for the Becketts to own a large property relatively near the city, and Foxrock was a popular place for a Dublin businessman to set up house. His mother, May, had been a nurse before her marriage; indeed, she first met Bill Beckett when he was a patient in the nursing home where she worked. On both sides, Beckett's immediate ancestors had been pillars of Dublin life. The Becketts were master builders, and the Roes (his mother's maiden name) had been involved in the grain trade. . . .

As he grew, Beckett gradually acquired the skills and habits common to a child of his age and class; he learned to swim, to play tennis, golf, chess and cricket, and to play the piano (the first indication of a lifelong interest in music). Neither was his education unique: from the age of five to the age of nine he attended a small, local school run by two sisters, the Misses Elsner (whose name and whose pet—a dog called Zulu—are used in the novel *Molloy*). Beckett's parents then sent him to a preparatory school, Earlsfort House, in Dublin: after Earlsfort House, Beckett followed his older brother first of all to Portora Royal School in Enniskillen in 1920, and then to the more prestigious of Dublin's two universities, Trinity College, in 1923. . . .

It was not until he entered Trinity in 1923 that Beckett began to fulfil his academic potential; and it was at Trinity, also, that he first encountered work that was to prove a lasting influence on his own writing. As an undergraduate Beckett studied French, a language he had begun to learn at his first school; at that time, the University stipulated that a student must study two languages, and Beckett accordingly chose Italian. The Professor of Romance Languages in Trinity at this time was Thomas Rudmose-Brown, who was to prove an important figure in Beckett's development both at and immediately after his time at Trinity. Beckett seems to have been a favourite of Rudmose-Brown's, although Beckett's thinly-disguised portraits of his old professor in his early work (Rudmose-Brown appears as the Polar Bear in both *Dream of Fair to Middling Women* and the story 'A Wet Night' in *More Pricks than Kicks*) demonstrate that he was not an uncritical admirer of his tutor. . . .

Psychological Problems Surface

It was during his time at Trinity that Beckett first began to suffer from the symptoms that were to plague him for most of his early adult life. From 1926 onwards, he was increasingly prone to what seems to have been a condition that was, at base, neurotic. His heart would race, making sleep impossible; later, his pounding heart would be supplemented by sweating and an accelerating sense of panic. In the later 1920s and 30s, these panic attacks would grow so severe that Beckett had to seek medical help.

As he neared the end of his undergraduate career, Beckett was at least clear about the direction he did not want his life to take. He did not want to work in the family business; nor did he want to be a clerk or a school-master, two other career paths that had been suggested to him by his family. The only option open to him was therefore to pursue the academic course that his success at Trinity had made possible. As a leading student in modern languages, Beckett was an obvious candidate for the year-long exchange programme that Trinity had organised with the École Normale Supérieure in Paris; the successful candidate would spend a year as a tutor at the École. . . .

The lecturer already in Paris, occupying (at least in Rudmose-Brown's eyes) the position that was rightfully Beckett's, was an older Irishman, Thomas MacGreevey. When Beckett eventually took up his position in Paris in 1928 MacGreevey was still at the École, and the two became friends. Thirteen years Beckett's senior, Mac-Greevey was an outgoing, convivial man; a poet as well as an academic, he had a wide interest in modern European art and literature, and also a pride in being Irish that the younger man found more difficult to accept (although both men disliked the increasingly restrictive atmosphere in the Irish Free State). MacGreevey can lay claim to being the most important contact that Beckett ever made. Not only did the young Beckett have regular friendly contact with someone who knew and could discuss literature and art, he also benefited from Mac-Greevey's knowledge of Parisian cultural life. Mac-Greevey's list of friends and contacts was profoundly impressive. He knew both W.B. Yeats and Jack Yeats, George Russell (A.E.), T.S. Eliot, James Stephens, and Richard Aldington; and, crucially, MacGreevey was part of the circle of friends, admirers and disciples that had gathered around the most feted and the most controversial Irish artistic exile, James Joyce.

Joyce's influence on Beckett is undoubtedly important, but it is in some respects hard to gauge. What seems undeniable is that Beckett came under Joyce's spell; he ran errands for the older writer, whose eyesight was failing. . . .

As one might expect, Joyce figured largely in the kind of work that the young Beckett found himself producing. His first commission, indeed, was for an essay on Joyce's *Work in Progress* (published as *Finnegans Wake*); the essay, 'Dante . . . Bruno. Vico . . . Joyce' was first published in 1929. At the same time, Beckett wrote his first short story, 'Assumption', and the poem that was to be his first independently published work, *Whoroscope*. In 1930, he received a further commission, for a monograph on [French novelist Marcel] Proust. This monograph was eventually published by Chatto and Windus, one of whose editors, Charles Prentice, supported Beckett through the 1930s. . . .

Kissing Cousins

By his early twenties, Beckett had grown into an attractive man; and, although his rather distant, reserved manner prevented him from forming easy relationships with women, he had, in the summer before he went to Paris, fallen in love with his cousin Peggy Sinclair. Peggy was the daughter of Beckett's maternal aunt Frances, also called Cissie, and his uncle William, who was known to his friends as Boss. . . .

However, by the winter of 1929, the love affair had waned. Peggy, it seems, was increasingly frustrated by Beckett's taciturn manner, and Beckett seems to have been uncomfortable both with Peggy's attitude to literature, and, if the largely autobiographical *Dream of Fair to Middling Women* is a truthful reflection of his state of mind, with Peggy's openly physical, sexual nature. Whatever the reason, by early 1930 the relationship had ended; it left its mark on his fiction, both in the lightly veiled character of the Smeraldina-Rima in his early work, and in references in *Krapp's Last Tape* to a girl in a green beret, whose memory Krapp invokes with a mingled melancholy and regret.

In Paris, Beckett had also drawn the attention of Joyce's daughter Lucia. Although Beckett admitted that he found Lucia attractive, her advances were unwelcome for a number of reasons; because of Peggy; because of Beckett's friendship with Joyce, which did not stretch to Joyce's family (with the exception of Joyce's son, Giorgio); and because of Lucia herself. By the late twenties, she was already displaying signs of the schizophrenia that would plague the rest of her life; her behaviour was, to say the least, variable, and she seemed unable to concentrate on any one task for very long.

Joyce, however, did not recognise his daughter's illness until her condition had deteriorated further; and when Beckett, in May 1930, finally told Lucia that he was not interested in her, Joyce and his wife took their daughter's side. The rift in Beckett's and Joyce's friendship was never absolute; but it did not truly heal until Joyce finally accepted the fact of his daughter's illness.

In September of that year, after delivering the manuscript of *Proust* to his publishers in London, Beckett returned to Dublin to take up a post in modern languages at Trinity. He had no choice (he was poor, and the post at Trinity was waiting for him), but he was not pleased at the prospect. . . .

Things Fall Apart

The illnesses that had first manifested themselves in his undergraduate days returned; he suffered from recurring cysts, was overly susceptible to colds (during 1931 he developed pleurisy) and he found himself once again prone to heart palpitations and night sweats. His life, for the moment, seemed to lack any direction; given this, his decision to resign from his lectureship at Trinity in 1932 was at least an attempt to deal with the growing crisis in his life, even though the decision, once taken, left him with a strong residue of guilt over the response of his parents and his old professor. . . .

[Eventually he returned] home, feeling increasingly isolated, and worked on his writing, producing, in addition to translations commissioned by [friend of James Joyce and publisher] Nancy Cunard, many of the stories later collected in *More Pricks*. His health worsened; the cysts returned, making an operation imperative, and Beckett entered [the] hospital in May 1933. The operation took place on the 3rd; on the same day, Peggy Sinclair died of tuberculosis in Germany. Her health had been failing for some time, but her death was still a considerable shock.

Worse was to come. Beckett, recuperating from the operation, found that his writing was drying up; depressed and frustrated, he began to drink heavily. . . . In mid-June, Bill suffered a major heart-attack; his younger son helped to take care of him, washing and shaving his father. At first, Beckett's father seemed to rally, but he had another, fatal heart attack on 26 June. . . .

> After my father's death I had trouble psychologically. The bad years were between when I had to crawl home in 1932 and after my father's death in 1933. I'll tell you how it was. I was walking down Dawson Street [in Dublin]. And I felt I couldn't go on. It was a strange experience I can't really describe. I found that I couldn't go on moving . . . and I felt I needed help. So I went to Geoffrey Thompson's surgery. . . . When he got there . . . he gave me a look over and found nothing physically wrong. Then he recommended psychoanalysis for me. Psychoanalysis was not allowed in Dublin at that time. It was not legal. So, in order to have psychoanalysis you had to come to London.

. . . In 1935 [the same year that his therapy ended],

Beckett began *Murphy*, the last of his novels to be set in a recognisable location (a minutely detailed London). To prepare for the novel, part of which was set in an asylum, Beckett accompanied his friend Geoffrey Thompson on his rounds at the Bethlem Royal Mental Hospital; other characters were formed in the same manner as those in *More Pricks*; in particular, the drunken bard Austin Ticklepenny was a potentially libellous portrait of Austin Clarke, an Irish poet known to Beckett. Stylistically, *Murphy* was an advance on Beckett's previous writing; it was clearer, sparer, and the arcane references of the earlier fiction were balanced by Beckett's dry, cool wit. . . .

At the end of 1937 Beckett learned that *Murphy* had finally finished its tour of publishers, and was to be brought out by Routledge (who had been shown the manuscript by Beckett's friend [painter and writer] Jack Yeats).

Between the signing of the contract and the novel's publication, Beckett's life took an unexpected and rather alarming turn. Beckett and an English couple, the Duncans (friends from his first trip to Paris in the 1920s) had been returning from a restaurant late at night, when a pimp, ironically named Prudent, fell into step beside them asking for money. Beckett refused; Prudent stabbed him, narrowly missing both his heart and his lung. The Duncans managed to move him to their flat; from there, the unconscious Beckett was taken to the Hospital Broussais. . . .

Samuel and Suzanne
Beckett's visitors in [the] hospital included a Frenchwoman, seven years his senior, named Suzanne Deschevaux-Dumesnil. The two had first met in the late 1920s, when Beckett was at the École; as Beckett recuperated, they spent an increasing amount of time together, and soon after he left [the] hospital they had de-

cided to live together. Suzanne was, by all accounts, something of a contradiction; strong and practical, but with a surprising belief in the unorthodox (she championed alternative medicine, for example), she was both generous to the underprivileged and sharply slighting of those she disliked. Her relationship with Beckett was not always an easy one; but she provided the stability that his life had lacked, and, crucially, she always believed in the value of his work. She was also a politically committed woman, with contacts in the French Communist Party; these contacts were to play a crucial role in Beckett's life in the first few years of the Second World War.

As war became inevitable, Beckett's dislike and distrust of the Nazis hardened; he had many Jewish friends who were directly threatened by a possible German invasion, and he soon realised that, in this case, 'you couldn't just stand by with your arms folded'. When the German army invaded France in May 1940 Beckett, who had already offered his services to the French authorities as an ambulance driver, initially decided to join the flood of people leaving Paris. He and Suzanne fled to Vichy, where Joyce and his family were now staying; this was to be Beckett's last meeting with the ailing Joyce, who died in January the following year. Joyce arranged a loan from his friend Valery Larbaud for the penniless couple; this helped to tide them over until Beckett's brother was able to arrange his allowance. They finally decided, however, to return to Paris; and once they arrived in the French capital, it was not long before they both became involved in the fledgling French Resistance.

The Joint War Effort

The cell they joined was codenamed Gloria SMH; it had been set up to organise the escape of British airmen who had been shot down over Paris, but by the time that Beckett and Suzanne joined it had become an information network, providing evidence of German troop movements for Allied intelligence. Beckett's job was one to which he was uniquely suited; he received information, translated it into English, compiling and editing a concise document that could be placed on microfilm and smuggled out of the country. The work was very dangerous. Although the group soon learned to be as secretive as possible there were many close calls, and the cell members found that, in practice, they could not ensure that security was as tight as they would like it to be. Beckett, Suzanne and the other members of the cell worked steadily through 1941; their luck deserted them the following year, when the cell was betrayed by a French priest, Fr Abeche, who had been recruited by the Germans. Beckett and Suzanne narrowly escaped Paris, and after a perilous journey through occupied France, they eventually found a safe refuge in the village of Roussillon, in the Vaucluse region of Vichy (a part of France nominally unoccupied, but in reality ruled by a puppet government on the Germans' behalf). . . .

Roussillon was liberated in 1945; Beckett's and Suzanne's first impulse was, understandably, to resume their lives in Paris. They quickly moved back to the apartment they had shared in the Rue des Favorites before the war, finding it miraculously untouched. . . .

A Creative Streak

From 1946 to 1953, . . . [Beckett] produced the works that were to establish him as an internationally famous writer. In a short, intense burst of writing he finished four lengthy short stories ('First Love', 'The Expelled', 'The Calmative' and 'The End'), four novels (*Mercier and Camier*, and the novels of the trilogy—*Malloy, Malone Dies*, and *The Unnamable*), and two plays (*Eleutheria*, and the play that more than any work has become identified with him, *Waiting for Godot*). The period is the more remarkable, because at its beginning Beckett was further away from literary fame than he had ever been. *Murphy* sold badly, and was remaindered; a French translation was prepared, but Beckett had his usual difficulty in finding a publisher for the manuscript. When Pierre Bordas finally took it on in October 1946, its sales were as disappointing as the English version's had been. *Watt* was doing the rounds of publishing firms to general incomprehension, even if Beckett's skill as a writer was at least acknowledged. . . .

Detailed Precision

His next play, *Endgame*, was begun in the aftermath of his [brother Frank's] death in 1955; at first, Beckett conceived of it as a two act play, but as the text was revised he slimmed it down, before arriving at its final form (a long one-act play). *Endgame* remained one of Beckett's favourite dramas; it was the first play to show, in great detail, the kind of care and attention to detail that he was to bring to his subsequent dramatic writing. But also, and perhaps unsurprisingly given the events in Beckett's life, the play is haunted by the prospect of universal death; the world outside Hamm's refuge is 'corpsed', and those inside the refuge seem eager to attain the same state (Clov: 'When I fall, I'll weep for happiness'). The same atmosphere hangs over another play, written at the same time; the radio script *All That Fall*, commissioned by the BBC, and delivered in September 1956. *All That Fall* is the most obviously autobiographical of Beckett's mature plays, at least in terms of its setting, which is, as Beckett himself noted, that of his childhood. . . .

In addition to *Endgame* and *All That Fall*, Beckett wrote the mime *Act Without Words* (1956), *Krapp's Last Tape* (1958), and the radio play *Embers* (1959). Each work relies for its effect, not only on the predicament of the characters, but on the increasingly sure and precise way in which the predicament is dramatised. . . .

He began his last full-length play *Happy Days* in 1960, taking meticulous care that the staging of the new work was as precise as he could make it; the text was substantially rewritten the following year, and was shown to an enthusiastic Alan Schneider, who offered to direct it in New York. As with *How It Is*, the play is something of a transitional work. *Happy Days*, like the plays that follow it, is built around a simple yet striking central image; it is also the first of Beckett's plays to be intricately patterned, with physical action balanced precisely against the spoken text. So closely did Beckett entwine the physical and verbal aspects of this and future texts, that any deviation from the text as printed would radically affect the production of the play. As productions of his texts proliferated, Beckett became notoriously exact about the director's fidelity to the text that he wrote. . . .

Marriage Without Bliss

He married Suzanne in England in 1960. This seems to have largely been for legal reasons; as he became wealthier, he began to worry about Suzanne's position should anything happen to him. The service was conducted in absolute secrecy, and only a very few of their friends knew of it. The marriage, however, did not change their relationship to any great extent; Beckett's life and Suzanne's diverged in some respects quite markedly. He never lost his sense of loyalty to his wife; but he began to have affairs, the longest lasting of which was with Barbara Bray, whom he met in London in the late 1950s. Their relationship lasted until Beckett's death, but there were others; and at certain points in the 1960s Suzanne came close to leaving him, claiming that the situation had become untenable. She did not; despite difficulties, they managed to retain enough in common for the marriage to survive.

In 1960 Beckett shared the Prix Formentor with the Argentinean author Jorge Louis Borges; and he began to be talked about as a potential candidate for the Nobel Prize. In 1969 came the news that he had won; he and Suzanne were holidaying in Tunisia when the news reached them, in the form of a telegram from Jerome Lindon

> Dear Sam and Suzanne. In spite of everything, they have given you the Nobel Prize—I advise you to go into hiding. With affection.

Beckett did not collect the award himself (he sent Lindon to Stockholm) and he dispersed the prize money amongst his needier friends. . . . The publicity associated with the Nobel seems to have been nothing more than an irritant to Beckett. His work had reached another impasse; and the added fame that the prize brought made even more demands on his time. . . .

Not I was the first of a series of plays that took the experiments of the 1960s to their conclusion; the tendency in the earlier plays toward patterned speech and movement, and toward an evocative rather than a dramatic text reaches its apogee in *Not I*, *That Time* (written in 1974), *Footfalls* (begun in 1975) and the plays that follow them. These texts are as brief as the rejected fragments of dramatic work that he produced in the 1960s (these are reprinted in the *Complete Dramatic Works* as *Rough for Theatre 1* and *2*), but they are as formally intricate and as austerely beautiful as anything that Beckett ever wrote.

Beckett's keen interest in the staging of his plays naturally led him towards direction. He began to stage his own texts in the 1960s, and in the 1970s he was used to receiving requests from theatres to supervise premieres and revivals of his work. He agreed only to a few of these requests, generally from actors and theatres that he knew. . . .

The Playwright's Final Years

Beckett continued to produce work almost until his death; the plays *Ohio Impromptu, Rockaby, A Piece of Monologue, Catastrophe* (dedicated to Vaclav Havel, the Czech dissident playwright) and *What Where;* the television plays *Quad* and *Nacht und Trame;* and *Stirrings Still*, his last prose work, finished in 1987. These late works are in the simple, spare style that he had developed for *Not I* and the late trilogy; they show no noticeable diminution of his skill as a writer. . . .

In 1986, he began to complain of difficulties in breathing; emphysema was diagnosed, and by the following year he could not travel any distance without using oxygen. In 1988, after a series of falls, he collapsed at home and was taken to hospital; although his condition was not definitely diagnosed, he seemed to be suffering from Parkinson's disease, the same illness that was responsible for his mother's death. His last work, the poem *what is the word*, was begun in hospital, and completed in the retirement home where he was to die the following year. . . .

Suzanne Beckett died on the 17th of April 1989; although their marriage had not been a particularly easy one, Beckett grieved for her. He did not outlive her long. He collapsed once more on the 6th of November 1989; on the 8th he was admitted to a neurological unit, after the initial tests for a suspected heart-attack had proved negative. Over the next few weeks he gradually drifted further and further into a coma, dying at 1 P.M. on the 22nd of December.

CHAPTER

5

Americans Address the Human Condition

Eugene O'Neill: A Psychologically Tortured Playwright

Maria T. Miliora

Eugene O'Neill (1888–1953) was perhaps more psychologically tortured by family trauma, emotional instability, and
grief in his life than any other great playwright. He was
born in New York to an alcoholic father and a mother who
became addicted to morphine right after his birth. The
same miseries that surface so graphically in O'Neill's autobiographical drama, *Long Day's Journey into Night*, were the
very plagues that sent him into deep depression and more
than once led to attempted suicide. O'Neill and his older
brother Jamie sank into alcoholism as young men—an addiction that O'Neill finally conquered at the age of thirty-
seven but one that took the life of Jamie. In adulthood,
O'Neill's relationships with his children were, for the most
part, distant and dysfunctional, and the patterns of depression, alcoholism, and suicide continued in this generation.

In the following excerpt from *Narcissism, the Family, and
Madness: A Self-Psychological Study of Eugene O'Neill and His
Plays*, Maria T. Miliora takes a hard look at the circum-

stances and relationships that so deeply affected O'Neill in his life and his writings. Miliora is a professor of organic chemistry and a lecturer in psychology at Suffolk University in Boston. She is a psychologist with a clinical practice in Boston and is a member of the senior faculty at the Training and Research Institute for Self Psychology in Manhattan. She has also written a book on film producer, director, writer, and actor Martin Scorsese.

❧   ❧   ❧

Eugene O'Neill was born in a Broadway, New York hotel, the Barrett House, on October 16, 1888. He was the third child and son born to Mary Ellen (Ella) Quinlan, and James O'Neill. Both parents were Catholics and of Irish descent.

James (b.1846) was a famous stage actor, known for his role as the Count of Monte Cristo. He was, at one time, considered a possible successor to Edwin Booth, but his greed cost him the development of his talent. *The Count of Monte Cristo* was very popular and it made James wealthy. He bought the rights to the play and portrayed the Count almost exclusively for the rest of his career.

Ella (b.1857), almost 12 years younger than James, was shy, sensitive, and apprehensive. Educated in a convent school and absorbed in music, she had considered becoming a nun. She had been close to her father, who drank himself into ill health and died of tuberculosis while she was still in school. When she met her future husband, she idealized the handsome actor. She married James in 1877, about three years after her father's death. She was 20, James was 31.

Both the O'Neill and Quinlan families had fled from Ireland during the mid–19th century. James O'Neill's father abandoned his wife and eight children and returned to Ireland when James was a child. He died from ingesting poison, but it is not clear whether his death was an accident or a suicide. James grew up in abject poverty and went to work at the age of ten to help support the family. He was the proverbial self-made man who achieved fame and wealth in spite of his humble beginnings. Ella's family had fared better in America. Her father had acquired some real estate, including a tobacco/liquor shop in Cleveland that was frequented by actors. It was in this shop that Ella and James met.

The reality of marriage to the actor did not measure up to Ella's romantic fantasies. They had no real home and the theatre was anything but glamorous. Theirs was a nomadic life, traveling from one theatre to another and living out of suitcases. Ella often spent nights alone in hotel rooms waiting for James, who usually returned very late, smelling of whiskey. Less than three months after their marriage, one of James's former girl friends sued him for divorce and claimed he was the father of her son. Although this claim could not be substantiated, the public accusation of sexual impropriety caused Ella anguish and shame.

Ella and James had a son, James Jr. (Jamie), born in 1878, and a second son, Edmund, was born in 1883. Once they had children, Ella tended to stay with them in a flat in New York while James traveled to his various appearances. But, because she and James could not bear long separations, sometimes she would leave her children in the care of her mother and join James.

The Death of a Brother

The second son, Edmund, died at about the age of eighteen months. This tragedy occurred after he contracted measles from Jamie. Ella had left the two boys with her mother in order to accompany her husband on the road. Jamie had been admonished not to go near the baby, but he did so, and the baby died while his mother was boarding a train to return home to attend to him. This event, and the guilt and recriminations that resulted from it, colored the family dynamics into which Eugene was born. The mother blamed herself, her husband, and her elder son for the baby's death. Jamie was sent to boarding school when he was seven, obviously affected by his sense of guilt and shame, and resentful of his father for separating him from his mother.

The second traumatic event that affected the O'Neill family was the birth of Eugene. This childbirth was difficult and debilitating for Ella and she was given morphine by a doctor to relieve her pain. Ella discovered that morphine eased her loneliness and anxiety as well, and she continued to use morphine after the boy's birth. She quickly became addicted to it. Ella's addiction affected the family and Eugene profoundly.

As a young child, Eugene and his mother toured with James, living in hotel rooms and backstage of his numerous performances. The parents hired a nanny, Sarah Sandy, who attended the youngster during his early years. Eugene was a sensitive and lonely child and he suffered from nightmares. Because of the constant traveling, Eugene had no companions and developed no peer relationships. Edmund's death contributed to Ella's being over-solicitous with her youngest son, whom she called "baby" even when he was an adult. Yet, particularly when she was in the throes of a morphine stupor, she was also distant and withdrawn.

The family spent summers in a cottage in New London, Connecticut, and this was the only home Eugene knew while he was growing up. His touring with his father during the first seven years of his life exposed him to the life of the theater, but it also left him feeling rootless. The constant comings and goings and the unpredictability of where he would be when he woke up mornings contributed to a lack of security that his basic physical and emotional needs would be met.

Off to Boarding School

When he was seven, Eugene was placed in a Catholic boarding school. This abrupt displacement from the familiar circle of his mother, father, and nurse to an unfamiliar world of strange children and nuns exacerbated his feelings of isolation, abandonment, and loneliness. Eugene did not even see his parents at Christmas because his father was performing. In one of his early sea plays, *The Long Voyage Home*, O'Neill describes the experience of a seaman, Olson, who is planning to return home but is drugged and shanghaied onto an alien ship. The sense of Olson's awakening in an alien world, far from his longed-for home and family, seems to capture O'Neill's own sense of abandonment. In the same fall of 1895, his brother, Jamie, who was now seventeen, began prep school.

According to [biographers Arthur and Barbara Gelb and Louis] Sheaffer, O'Neill was very lonely as a boy and he developed a love for two solitary activities— reading and swimming. Both of his parents were distant figures. His mother, because of her addiction, was emotionally unresponsive at least some of the time; his father was an idealized, overwhelming, heroic figure on a stage. Moreover, although he idealized his brother, he rarely saw him except during their summers together.

In 1897, when Eugene was nine years old, a second paternity suit was filed against his father by the son of the girl friend who had sued James years before. This distressed the family for some three years before James defeated the suit. Eugene's brother, Jamie, who blamed himself for the dead brother's death and his mother's problems, was asked to leave college a few months before his graduation for bringing a prostitute into the school. Ella was sometimes away for long periods in sanitoria, but Eugene did not understand why his mother was ill. At about the age of eleven or twelve, Eugene knew that there was something wrong with his mother and he feared she might be mentally ill. When he asked his father and brother about his mother's strange behavior, he was told that his mother had a kind of sickness.

When Eugene was twelve, he was enrolled in another Catholic school and lived with his parents in a New York hotel. According to Sheaffer, "when Eugene was around thirteen he overheard his mother confiding to someone that she had been against having her last child, that it had been her husband's desire that they should have another one." In this way Eugene learned that he had been unwanted by his mother.

Later in his adolescence, at about the age of fifteen, Eugene discovered that his mother was addicted to morphine. It happened that his mother ran out of morphine during a storm while the family was together in the summer cottage. Ella, tormented by the craving for the drug, dashed out of the house in her nightdress and tried to throw herself into the river. Her sons and husband raced after her and stopped her. James and Jamie explained to Eugene that her behavior was due to morphine addiction, and that she had been given the drug initially during his birth. Eugene's religious faith, which had been wavering for some time, was now forsaken entirely. Thereafter, he attended Betts Academy, a nonsectarian boarding school, during his adolescent years.

According to Sheaffer, Jamie's reaction to the death of Edmund as well as Ella's addiction was one of intensified devotion to her and hatred for his father. He attributed his mother's problems to his father's using a "quack" doctor at the time of Eugene's birth and to their constant traveling. After his education was terminated, he assumed an acting career of sorts but remained financially dependent on his father. Moreover, he became a chronic drunk and spent much of his time gambling and whoring.

O'Neill Hits the Bottle

Eugene began drinking sometime in his fifteenth year, soon after he discovered his mother's addiction, with his older brother serving as guide. Jamie also introduced Eugene to avant-garde literature and his first prostitute.

At seventeen (1906), Eugene graduated from school with no ambition or goals. Pressured by his father to attend college, he went to Princeton for one year (1906–1907), but he spent more time drinking than he did studying. He also experimented with drinking absinthe, a wormwood-alcohol intoxicant that is a particularly potent neurotoxic. He was expelled from Princeton for pranks and cutting classes. He worked briefly as a secretary in a supply company during 1908–1909, a job his father found for him, and he wrote poetry while sharing a studio in New York with two artists.

O'Neill met Kathleen Jenkins in the spring of 1909, when both were twenty, and they apparently fell in love and had sexual relations. Soon thereafter, he sought to extricate himself from his involvement and appealed to his father for help. James proposed that Eugene join a mining engineer who was planning to take a trip to Spanish Honduras to prospect for gold. The ship was due to sail from San Francisco. Eugene told Kathleen of his plans, and they married secretly (on October 2, 1909) before his departure.

When O'Neill returned, he joined his father, who opened in *The White Sister* during March 1910. Soon thereafter, the marriage to Jenkins and the birth of his son, Eugene O'Neill, Jr. (born May 7, 1910), were revealed by Kathleen's mother. O'Neill avoided seeing his wife and baby and, instead, during June 1910, he sailed to Buenos Aires. The trip was sanctioned and financed by his father both because he wanted Eugene to distance himself from Kathleen and he hoped the trip would help Eugene to mature.

Apparently, O'Neill found great contentment on board the ship, and he had cordial relations with the crew. In Argentina, he became a real down-and-outer, often out of work and without money, sleeping on park benches, and alone. He sailed for home in March 1911 as a shiphand on a freighter and arrived in New York on the night of April 15, having been away for almost a year. He returned home, having absorbed a store of rich experiences but feeling as unsettled as before. These experiences would find expression, later, in his sea plays.

O'Neill frequented "Jimmy the Priest's," a saloon and flophouse, and the "Hell Hole," and he went off to sea another time. He returned to New York in mid-September 1911 and went to the flophouse. There, he received word from Kathleen that she wanted a divorce. She did not want alimony or child support, only evidence of adultery since this was the only permissible grounds for obtaining a divorce. To satisfy this request, O'Neill arranged to be seen in bed with a prostitute as evidence of adultery. This episode left him feeling humiliated and degraded.

An Attempt at Suicide

In January 1912, at twenty-three, Eugene attempted suicide by an overdose of Veronal sleeping tablets (an opiate) while he was staying at "Jimmy the Priest's." He was in a deep depression at the time and his attempts to use alcohol to uplift his mood were unsuccessful. O'Neill was found in a coma by one of the roomers, who, together with others at the flophouse, took turns walking O'Neill until the effects of the Veronal wore off. According to Sheaffer, O'Neill wanted desperately to become a poet, feeling that this was the one hope he had for his life. But he had limited ability for writing poetry. After the suicide attempt, O'Neill returned to his family and had a brief fling in vaudeville.

O'Neill worked as a reporter on a New London newspaper, another job his father obtained for him, during August of 1912. In New London he courted Maibelle Scott. Soon thereafter, he became ill and was diagnosed as having pleurisy. He was nursed at home for some months, and his mother's response to his illness was increased use of morphine. She was tormented by the loss of another son as well as by memories of her father's death from tuberculosis. According to Sheaffer, "there was a side of him that enjoyed his illness; reduced to a feeling of dependency and brought into closer contact with his mother than in years, he reacted by becoming childlike." In December 1912, he entered the Fairfield County State Tuberculosis Sanatorium, a hospital for paupers, but he remained for only two days. A short time later, he was admitted to the Gaylord Farm Sanatorium in Wallingford, Connecticut. It was at Gaylord, during the first half of 1913, that he began to write plays.

O'Neill rejoined his family in New London during June of 1913. He remained in New London through the winter, rooming at the home of his neighbors, the Rippins. He continued to date Maibelle Scott, but by spring of 1914, he had left the Rippin household and had ended his romance with Maibelle. That spring, Ella cured herself of her addiction by staying in a religious convent for an extended period. By that time, at the age of 26, Eugene was writing plays which were coming out of his mind and onto paper quickly and easily. During the first two years of his writing career (1913–1915), O'Neill turned out eleven plays. Most of these include characters who meet violent death by murder or suicide.

A Playwriting Career Begins

During 1914–1915, O'Neill was engaged to another woman, Beatrice Ashe, and he took a course in playwriting taught by Professor [George Pierce] Baker at Harvard. By mid-1916, Ashe had broken their engagement and Eugene turned to drinking heavily. In 1916, he joined an avant-garde group of writers who had established an amateur theatre company, the Provincetown Players. O'Neill's first one-act plays were performed by this group in Provincetown, Cape Cod. As a result of this association, O'Neill began his playwriting career as part of an enterprise that was created by bohemian artists, who rebelled against the commercialism and old-fashioned theatricality that James O'Neill had known.

During 1916, O'Neill met Agnes Boulton, a writer, and in 1918, when he was twenty-nine, they were married. O'Neill and Agnes had two children, Shane, born in 1919, and Oona, in 1925. Among the better known plays O'Neill wrote during 1916 were *Moon of the Caribbees* and *Ile* and, during the 1918–1919 period, he wrote his first full-length play, *Beyond the Horizon*.

Eugene O'Neill suffered from depression, he was phobic about crowds, and he was an alcoholic. His close friend, George Jean Nathan, described him as taciturn, given to brooding, and stated that his "dislike of meeting people . . . amounts almost to a terror.". . .

The period of the early 1920s was a particularly turbulent time for O'Neill. In 1920, *Beyond the Horizon* opened and he was awarded his first Pulitzer prize. His father suffered a stroke and was diagnosed with intestinal cancer. The elder O'Neill died on August 10, 1920, in New York. Eugene spent time at his father's bedside and was moved by his tortured, last days.

Other plays from this period include *The Emperor Jones, Anna Christie, The First Man, The Hairy Ape,* and *Welded. Welded* seems to capture aspects of his relationship with Agnes. In the play, both the male and female characters are locked in a polarized, intense, love-hate relationship. The character, Michael Cape, is a writer, his wife, Eleanor, is an actress, and both are selfish and self-centered. There are scenes in which they are very close physically, but, nevertheless, are not able to hear each other (that is, they are utterly unempathic with one another). The closeness-distance and love-hate dynamics between the characters are depicted as extreme polarities.

After the death of his father, Jamie stopped drinking and became his mother's companion. Early in 1922, Jamie and Ella traveled to California to inspect some investment property that had been purchased by James. Ella was felled by a stroke, and a brain tumor was discovered. Jamie was distraught, he began drinking again at a feverish rate, and he wired his brother to come to the Coast. Eugene wired back that he was unwell, a claim the veracity of which Sheaffer questions. Ella died, February 28, 1922, and the coffin bearing her body and a totally intoxicated Jamie traveled by train back to New York. Eugene failed to meet the train, having become agitated about the prospect of doing so. He attended the funeral, but Jamie did not because he was too drunk. Jamie continued his self-destructive course, seemingly wishing to drink himself to death, and he died as a result of his alcoholism in a sanatorium on November 8, 1923.

During the early to mid-1920s, O'Neill produced several plays of note. These include *All God's Chillun Got Wings, Desire Under the Elms,* and *The Great God Brown,* as well as others which were less well-received.

O'Neill Conquers His Drinking Problem

O'Neill went on a particularly long and destructive drinking binge on the one-year anniversary of his brother's death. In the mid-twenties, O'Neill had six weeks of treatment by Gilbert Hamilton, a psychoanalyst in New York City, who was conducting research on the sexual practices of married couples. Among his subjects were Eugene O'Neill and Agnes Boulton. After this experience with Hamilton, early in 1926, O'Neill stopped drinking. He was 37. He remained essentially sober, except for brief lapses, for the rest of his life.

O'Neill began a relationship with Carlotta Monterey in 1926, and he abandoned Agnes and his children at Spithead (Bermuda) in December of 1927. He traveled to Europe with Carlotta during February 1928, trying to escape from the publicity generated by the affair and hoping to begin a new life. He suffered emotional distress over the acrimony between him and Agnes that was generated by the divorce. He married Carlotta in Paris in July 1929, and they did not return to the United States until 1931.

O'Neill's plays during this period include *Strange Interlude* (1926–1927), *Dynamo* (1924–1928), and *Days Without End* (1927–1933), *Mourning Becomes Electra* (1929–1931), and *Ah, Wilderness!* (1932). . . .

After O'Neill left his family in Bermuda in 1927, he never again lived with his children, although they sometimes visited him. He barely knew his daughter, Oona, disapproved of her going to Hollywood, and disowned her when she married Charles Chaplin in 1943. He met his firstborn son, Eugene Gladstone O'Neill 2nd, in 1921 when the boy was about twelve and they developed a relationship. The younger O'Neill received a doctorate from Yale and became a respected classics scholar, receiving an appointment as an assistant professor at Yale. The life events of the younger O'Neill, however, indicate a lack of stability and a propensity for depression and fragmentation. He was married three times, had an emotionally explosive relationship with the last woman with whom he lived, and he left his academic position for a career in radio. He drank heavily and committed suicide in 1950 by slashing his wrists. He was 40 years old.

O'Neill's abandonment of his family in 1927 was particularly difficult on Shane, who was about eight years old at the time. Not unlike O'Neill as a boy, Shane was sensitive and lonely, and he never found stability either in schools or in a career. Shane married and he and his wife had a child, Eugene Gladstone III, who died during infancy, apparently due to suffocation. Shane abused alcohol and marijuana, became a heroin addict, and was arrested for heroin possession. O'Neill disowned him, as he had Oona. Shane committed suicide in 1977.

During the latter phase of his writing career, O'Neill began a series of "cycle" plays whose aim was to depict the country's history through an intergenerational family chain. O'Neill destroyed most of this unfinished work shortly before his death. His last completed works—*The Iceman Cometh, Hughie, Long Day's Journey into Night*, and *A Moon for the Misbegotten*—are considered milestones in American dramaturgy.

O'Neill won four Pulitzers (*Beyond the Horizon; Anna Christie; Strange Interlude;* and *Long Day's Journey into Night* [posthumously]), and he was awarded the Nobel Prize for literature in 1936. A tremor that had been with him from the time he was a schoolboy grew increasingly worse, and by 1943 he could no longer write longhand. Unfortunately, he was never able to find a substitute for writing in this way and, during the last several years of his life, he was a virtual invalid. The tremor was considered a symptom of Parkinson's Disease, but after O'Neill's death, an autopsy indicated that this diagnosis was not correct. It was determined that there was degeneration of the cerebellum, which destroyed the motory system, but the disorder was unnamed.

Several other illnesses plagued O'Neill, particularly during the latter phase of his life. He and Carlotta took pain-killing and sedative drugs, and both may have suffered from bromide poisoning in 1951. The tragedies surrounding his children, his inability to write, and his illness that rendered him an invalid deepened his depression during the last years of his life. He died on November 27, 1953, in the Hotel Shelton in Boston at the age of 65.

Thornton Wilder: Adapter of Writing Styles and Modes

David Castronovo

Thornton Wilder (1897–1975) was born in Madison, Wisconsin, but spent some of his youth in China, where his father held the consul general post in Hong Kong. The young Wilder, who moved between two continents, was alternately influenced by a solicitous, Calvinist father and an imaginative, art-loving mother. He graduated from Yale University and received his master's degree from Princeton University. He became a popular teacher and lecturer, holding posts at a boarding school in New Jersey, the University of Chicago, and Harvard University.

Wilder's body of literary work is not as voluminous as that of many other writers, in part because he became disillusioned with his own writing styles. But the modes he adapted for his novel *The Bridge of San Luis Rey* (1927) and for his plays *Our Town* (1938) and *The Skin of Our Teeth* (1942) won him three Pulitzer Prizes. Wilder was a modernist writer whose stories centered on such themes as economic depression, fire, pestilence, and war.

In this excerpt from the book *Thornton Wilder*, author David Castronovo provides a look at Wilder, the man of letters. Castronovo, who is a critic, an essayist, and an asso-

David Castronovo, *Thornton Wilder*. New York: Ungar, 1986. Copyright © 1986 by the Ungar Publishing Company. Reproduced by permission.

ciate professor of English at Pace University in New York City, has published several books, including a *New York Times* notable book, *Edmund Wilson*, in 1984. In recent years he has collaborated with scholar Janet Groth on the uncollected works and correspondence of Wilson.

🐝   🐝   🐝

[T]hornton] Wilder's early life and its conflicts foreshadow the complex and problematic nature of his work: cheerful submission to authority and the yearning for adventure and exoticism, Americanism and the attraction of European culture, Protestant rectitude and aestheticism—these are the themes that take the field both in childhood and later life. Amos Wilder, the author's father, had been reared in Maine and bred up to the Calvinist mission of dedication to public causes, devotion to family life, and avoidance of frivolity. A sententious man of his time, Amos embodied the faults of the up-and-doing professional: distrust of the arts, rigidity, censoriousness, and love of high-flown pronouncements about man's inner life. A Yale graduate and Ph.D. in political science, he began a career as a teacher before switching to journalism. Marriage and family life started at the time he bought an interest in a Madison, Wisconsin, newspaper. Amos became the scourge of corrupt politicians and the liquor interests. As husband and father he began a fairly typical reign as a benign bully—indoctrinating, intimidating, and condemning—but doing so in a genial tone of voice. The newspaper income soon proved inadequate to meet the needs of a growing family, but a good connection brought Amos a post as consul general in Hong Kong.

Of the Wilder children—Thornton, Amos, Janet,

Charlotte, and Isabel—Thornton Niven, born in Wisconsin in 1897, was the greatest source of anxiety for "Papa." The record of Wilder's childhood was filled with gentle paternal admonitions: Thornton's "artistic temperament," his dreamy irresponsibility, his oddity of manner and self-absorption alarmed Amos. Papa pronounced Thornton's early literary efforts to be "carving on olive pits." He hoped that Thornton would not "lay too much stress on Greek or any other plays. I must hold that the man who does a thing is more important than the fellow who shows how it is done." Sometimes he was even pleased with the young boy: "I rejoice that Thornton is able to water an occasional lawn."

Bounced Between the West and the East

Thornton was also subjected to shifts from school to school. After starting his education in Madison, he was brought to Hong Kong in 1906 and enrolled in a German school. Wilder's mother, an imaginative woman of taste and culture who had been frustrated as a young girl in her aspirations to study medicine, disliked everything about the China arrangements; the constant social obligations and her fears about educational prospects for the children soon drove her back to the States—this time to Berkeley, California. Thornton now took part in little-theater productions and studied music. But by 1909 Papa summoned the family, except for brother Amos, back to China. Thornton and his sister Charlotte were sent to the China Inland Mission Boys and Girls School in Chefoo, an institution that emphasized classics and muscular Christianity—including compulsory cricket (a game from which Wilder got himself exempt). Here he met Henry Luce, the future *Time* mogul. He developed a rather lively personality and a reputation for being eccentric.

When Thornton was sixteen, another change came.

He left China to attend the Thacher School, a fancy prep school where he continued to polish his reputation as an oddity, an arty type, and drama enthusiast. (Papa, [biographer] Gilbert Harrison reports, would not permit Thornton to play the part of Lady Bracknell in [Oscar Wilde's] *The Importance of Being Earnest*). In 1913 still another adjustment was made—Berkeley High School and home life with his mother and sisters. The home—minus Papa—was now dominated by Mrs. Wilder and her love of European culture and art. Thornton discovered modern writers like [Marcel] Proust and [Thomas] Mann, became an avid theatergoer, and shared his ardors with a mother whom he referred to as "Our Lady of Florence." He also conceived of a series of three-minute plays that he worked on during his college years. His conceptions were exotic and atypical of most teenage literary enterprises: instead of writing about personal experience, he chose to create a strange, nonreferential world of fantasies. One of these plays takes place inside a Renaissance painting; another is set in Saint Francis's Italy. . . .

College Years

When Wilder finished high school, Amos presented the next surprise—not Yale, but Oberlin College [in Ohio]. The grander institution was considered to be too worldly and sophisticated for the poorly disciplined and vaguely focused boy. Oberlin—a Congregationalist plain-living-and-high-thinking college—was more to Papa's taste; it satisfied Thornton too. The peculiar richness of Oberlin—with its compulsory Chapel, fine humanistic curriculum, and social progressivism—was very accessible to a boy whose father was a Puritan do-gooder and whose mother was a culture seeker. . . .

With Papa at a distance, the young man . . . socialized a great deal and spent more time on his writing than on course work. The results showed in a mediocre academic record. At the end of his second year, another shift came: Amos decided to send "hopeless Thornton" to Yale. When he started at New Haven, without Junior status because of the weak grades, the academic situation was the same: writing at the expense of studying. While juggling a demanding program as an English major, he pursued such extracurricular gratifications as the Elizabethan Club and the *Lit*—the first a social paradise for a writer in search of talk, the second a place to publish his one-act plays. Papa, meanwhile, had Thornton paying his dues to the workaday world: the student went several nights a week to study business subjects at a local institute. On top of that, Thornton started writing and reviewing for a New York paper; this led to running to the city and wandering around Greenwich Village. And then one of the besetting problems of his life appeared—his love of exciting company. The transfer student from the Midwest came under the influence of the more glamorous Yale types. The writer who dissipated so much time in the 1930s and 1940s with New York literary people began his social career among the well-born and cultivated undergraduates. He was impressed by the "golden casualness" of young men who traveled with [poet, radio playwright, and author] Stephen Vincent Benét, bought deluxe-edition books, and seemed to belong at Oxford. . . .

At Yale, he won the Bradford Brinton Award for *The Trumpet Shall Sound*, a play suggested by Ben Jonson's *The Alchemist*. This allegory of possession and justice, about what happens when servants take over their master's house, is interesting for its moralistic emphasis and its frank use of another playwright's material. During the Yale years he also worked on the three-minute plays. Some of these efforts are rather heavily and indigestibly flavored with biblical, medieval, and fin de siècle styles.

Clearly, a practical man like Amos did not know what to do with a son involved in such experiments. World War I had briefly interrupted Thornton's Yale career and caused him to spend some time in the Coast Guard at Newport [Rhode Island]. But what would the "dear boy" do with his life? Fortunately for Thornton, his mother came up with the idea of a year of study at the American Academy in Rome. Amos provided nine hundred dollars for the year, and Thornton then set off on a budget version of the American gentleman's postgraduate tour of the Old World. In Rome he acquired a light coating of Latin and archaeology and gained entrance to a few salons. Gilbert Harrison reports that there was a powerful romantic experience with a woman—and a painful rejection that is later registered in his first novel, *The Cabala*. During his year abroad, Wilder did not acquire the tastes and attitudes of the expatriates. After a while, he even longed for home and his father's authority: "Your queer 'aesthetic,' over-cerebral son may yet turn out to be your most fundamental New Englander." Papa, of course, wanted the trip to pay: he searched up a job as a French teacher at the Blairstown School and sent Thornton to Paris to prepare by studying the language. Living on ninety cents a day, Thornton got a mere taste of literary France, including visits to cafés, calls on his Yale friends, and a stop at Sylvia Beach's Shakespeare and Company.

The Joys of Teaching

When he returned to the States, the teaching appointment turned out to be at Lawrenceville School. As a job, it was a considerable source of satisfaction; he became a popular, dedicated teacher and housemaster. The man of European tastes enjoyed helping his students by tutoring, advising, and even doing day-to-day tasks like chauffeuring and monitoring. While other members of his generation were escaping Anglo-Saxon America, Wilder seemed to be moving on a different path: "There is no longer any sense of incompleteness or strangeness about any pleasure I get out of America." And yet the creative activity of the period, especially *The Cabala* and *The Bridge of San Luis Rey*, suggests a strange mental distance from the concerns of his New Jersey colleagues and students. While working as a prep-school master, he was voyaging in Rome and Peru.

Thornton started the 1920s in Europe, moved to New Jersey, and ended in Europe: during the middle stretch of time, he became a celebrity. *The Bridge of San Luis Rey* brought immediate fame and money, but it did not represent any radical departure from Wilder's earlier efforts or any attempt to write popular fiction. This highly wrought, exquisite book was a predictable second novel for the writer who had published a very literary first novel. The first work, originally to be called *Memoirs of a Roman Student* and later changed to *The Cabala*, is about a group of self-absorbed patricians, each enmeshed in a special kind of frustration. Begun at Lawrenceville, the novel was finished during a two-year leave of absence from the school, a period during which Wilder had decided to take an M.A. [master of arts degree] in romance languages at Princeton. The book has the aroma of scholarship combined with the delicate craftsmanship of a series of miniature portraits. . . .

The Bridge, coming promptly in 1927, is similarly fabricated: Wilder of course had never seen Peru and had spent most of his time during the period with New Yorkers, his family, and his Lawrenceville charges. He conjured up three portraits of unsuccessful lovers and then framed them with an ironic discussion of why these pathetic romantics died on the same day (in the first draft, the date was Wilder's birthday) in a catastrophic accident. . . .

Wilder [turned] to America in two of his greatest one-act plays, *The Happy Journey to Trenton and Camden* and *Pullman Car Hiawatha*. These works are the first of many important returns to the States, but like later ones—*Our Town, The Eighth Day*—they are far different from the work of the local colorist or the social chronicler. Both plays effectively present time passing and people's epiphanies as they are sped through stylized landscapes. Using his eye to create settings that are so typical that they are terrifying, he accelerates his people—on a train and in a car—through the ordinary joys and agonies of all places and times. . . .

His next book was the *Woman of Andros* (1930), a novel set in the first century A.D. The work was a flash point in his career, a quiet and suavely written narrative that set off a reaction out of proportion to its worth or its shortcomings. . . .

A Caustic Critic

But eight months after the book was published in 1930, the first major crisis of his career came in the form of a review in the liberal *New Republic*. Mike Gold, an editor of the left-wing *New Masses*, had been asked by acting editor Malcolm Cowley to write a guest review. Although [critic, journalist, historian, and novelist] Edmund Wilson had offered his characteristic reasoned guidance, Gold greeted Wilder's third novel—and by extension his first two—with a meat axe. In the heated-up prose of the Communist ideologue, Gold accused Wilder's work of being effete and irresponsible. . . . Gold put together an attack that combined open invective and innuendo: "Wilder: Prophet of the Genteel Christ" refers to the novelist as "The Emily Post of Culture"; the Greek characters in *The Woman of Andros* are called "homosexual figures in graceful gowns moving archaically among the lilies.". . .

Meanwhile, Wilder's life in the 1930s was congested with university commitments [he taught classics in translation and advanced composition at the University of Chicago], public lecturing, and family responsibilities. He suffered a mild breakdown in 1935, a setback that required his leaving the university and, tired and troubled as he was, dashing to Europe. The problem seemed to be a career crisis combined with certain private burdens that aggravated his writing worries. Papa died in 1936 and "the protracted exasperating unloveable death" left Wilder with a sense that he had not done enough for the solicitous parent. Soon after, Wilder was in Vienna paying a call on [neurologist and psychologist Sigmund] Freud. In the great man's study he had a chance to get another response to his work. Freud did not like *Heaven's My Destination*, both because of its religious concerns and what he considered the author's flippancy about the serious question of human illusions. . . .

The Vienna visit must have been an anxious occasion on which [Wilder's] problems converged. Wilder needed some release from the pain, constraint, and needling comments of family and critics. He also needed a way out of his "type" of novel—the delicately crafted work of sensibility and ironic distance.

A Playwright Is Born

"Why don't you write a play?" Norman Bel Geddes, the theater designer, suggested. A full-length drama was an attractive project, yet a daunting undertaking for a writer who had not done a long dramatic work since his Yale days. *Our Town*—written very slowly and with great enthusiasm—was the response to the suggestion and the confrontation of his 1930s crisis. It inaugurated a playwriting period that proved successful until the early 1940s. The play brought with it deep personal satisfaction, public recognition, and a Pulitzer Prize. . . .

The Merchant of Yonkers, a farcical look at humanity's struggle for pleasure and joy, appeared in 1939. An adaptation of a work by the Austrian playwright [Johann] Nestroy, which Wilder replanted in the New York of the 1880s, the play was the first version of *The Matchmaker* and the script on which *Hello, Dolly!* was eventually based. As it was metamorphosed during Wilder's lifetime, through his revisions and through the efforts of composer lyricist Jerry Herman in the musical comedy, the play lost its sharp critical edge and became just another commercial entertainment. The sly and playful spirit of the original version of *The Merchant of Yonkers* warmed Wilder up for his greatest comic work, *The Skin of Our Teeth*. *The Merchant* is a bridge between two plays about destiny, time, and endurance: it is the connective between the tragic vision of *Our Town* and the reconstitutive spirit of *The Skin of Our Teeth*.

In the late 1930s, Wilder began to give a good deal of time to writing about the ways in which he encountered literature and art. Now part of the public record of Wilder's achievement as a writer and intellectual, *The Journals of Thornton Wilder 1939–1961* offer a rich sampling of ideas and impressions of literature, philosophy, and the arts and an account—often cheerful, but sometimes distressed and frustrated—of the artist's works in progress. His wide-ranging scholarly interests—motifs in [Renaissance composer Giovanni da] Palestrina, the dating of Lope de Vega's plays, the text of [James Joyce's] *Finnegans Wake*, the defining qualities of classic American authors, techniques in [Charles] Dickens, Stendhal, [Miguel de] Cervantes, [economist and philosopher] Thorstein Veblen's failings as a thinker—make this document an extraordinary one, especially if one measures Wilder's explorations against those of his contemporaries in America. As a playwright and novelist, he was certainly equipped with curiosity that no other peer could rival. And *The Journals* show the process by which he enriched and transformed his own stage and fictional plans through the use of other writers' visions. [Franz] Kafka, [Søren] Kierkegaard, [Jean] Genet, [Jean-Paul] Sartre, the philosophes, [Thomas] Mann, [Giovanni] Boccaccio, the Greeks, Zen Buddhism: his unfailing appetite for literature, art, and thought takes the form of a delight in deriving—typically, a passage about an author will tell about a motif that Wilder wanted for his own work. *The Journals* chronicle these literary experiences for some twenty-two years. . . .

In Service to America
Before *The Skin* was produced in 1942, Wilder was occupied with several nonliterary jobs—the latest examples of his tendency to follow Papa's advice about practical work. In 1941, before Pearl Harbor, he assumed a State Department position as a goodwill ambassador to several South American countries. The mission was a matter of cocktail hours, soirées, speeches, and readings—everything that could distract a writer from his work. When the war broke out, he volunteered and was accepted into Army Air Intelligence: he loved the immersion in the nonliterary and enjoyed "being pure instrument, however modestly, in a movement." Here at least he had found an uncomplicated authority to submit himself to. He wrote little or nothing from 1942 to 1945.

During the war, there was a corrosive criticism gnawing at Wilder's reputation. *The Skin of Our Teeth* opened on Broadway in 1942 at a time when Captain Wilder had barely assumed his duties. On leaves, the author scuttled between his Washington post and New York rehearsals. . . . The production—with Tallulah Bankhead playing the maid-seductress Sabina in a careening and uncontrolled style—was threatening to run off with the text and disappear into the realms of burlesque. Wilder's ironic collage of images and situations was in the hands of egomaniacs. But the worst part of the *Skin* experience came a month after the play opened to generally favorable reviews. The critics' axe swung again, this time in a *Saturday Review of Literature* article by two Joyce scholars, Joseph Campbell and Henry Morton Robinson. Wilder was accused of plagiarizing Joyce's *Finnegans Wake*. Preposterous as the charge was, it did seem to connect with Wilder's special interests: for years he had been poring over Joyce's text—and he certainly did borrow several of Joyce's methods including conflation of time, mixing of images, cyclic patterning, and finding correspondences between the lives of ancient and modern man. But the accusation is the more outrageous for being insensitive to the nature of dramatic art: Joyce's work is wholly without the page-to-page conflict and character-building that is the playwright's contribution to literature. Wilder's play also had its own humor, settings, and social vision. . . .

A Dry Spell

Except for *The Ides of March*, published in 1948, and a few extraordinary plays produced in the early 1960s, the twenty years after the war were filled with forced work and false starts, strewn with abandoned projects, and occupied with the busy work of literature rather than the passion of creating. The attacks on the use of models struck at the roots of Wilder's art. Fortunately he did not abandon his intense involvement with past literature, but he did fall prey to a certain panic, depression, and miscalculation. . . .

In the forties Wilder was working on a three-act play called *The Emporium*. Set in an American department store, the drama had its origins in Wilder's attraction to Franz Kafka's *The Castle*, particularly to the themes of mysterious human institutions and man's futile search for coherence. The *Journals* now tell us the full story—genesis, influences, struggles, frustrations, abandonment. Apparently Wilder wanted to combine the unsettling quality of Kafka's story with—it seems hard to believe—a Horatio Alger motif [a plucky hero]. About a young man who wants to "belong" to the labyrinthine world of a strange department store, the plot thread is complicated by Wilder's involvement with Kierkegaard's angst, Saint John of the Cross's "dark night of the soul," and his own ideas about transcendence. In the attempt to harmonize unharmonizeable elements, he only managed to tangle himself up for years: disillusioned with his own techniques in *Our Town* and *The Skin of Our Teeth*, he sought a new kind of "originality" in his fusions. The result is a collection of pages with interesting motifs, prose commentaries, and half-formulated plans. . . .

For a famous writer who has lost the visionary gleam, there are always public enterprises. The most enervating of these was Wilder's 1950 appointment as Charles Eliot Norton lecturer in American literature at Harvard; this academic plum turned out to be a source of frustration. At first it seemed stimulating—filled with parties, new research possibilities, great students. But the obligation to publish lectures on classic American authors like [Herman] Melville and [Edgar Allan] Poe was hardly a minor responsibility. And, as Gilbert Harrison has suggested, Wilder's mind was most at home with narrative forms, not with exposition and argument. Wilder loved to seek large generalizations, but not in the form of essays. The Norton lectures hung over him for years, like some unpleasant student task that must be completed. . . .

Honorary degrees poured in, but little distinguished work was finished in the 1950s. Amos Wilder, the author's brother, speaks of Thornton's "total humanistic

outreach" as it involves other things than writing—
"This artist's role included all such gregariousness, involvement, pedagogy, and missions." Although a noble
rationalization, this remark cannot really convince us
that Wilder was not frustrated and hampered by
celebrity status as well as by his own self-indulgence
and impatience with difficult work. Wilder even confessed to a "vast accumulated self-discontent" about his
desultory work methods. Grand designs about a play
cycle were formed—the new title was to be "The Seven
Ages of Man." But only *Infancy* and *Childhood*, two fine,
ironic plays, were to be completed. The old freedom
and imagination were on display in these little dramas,
and also in *Someone from Assisi*, but there was no evidence that Wilder was entering a period of intense productivity. A fascinating project called *The Sandusky
Mystery Play*, a small-town pageant that tried to experi-
ment with stage technique, is reminiscent of *Our Town*
and the feeling for the particularity of life evinced in
that work. But the play was dropped—a symbolic failure suggesting Wilder's disillusionment with his own
best modes. . . .

A Second Wind

Wilder moved beyond this impasse and regained his
footing by returning to fiction. In 1963 he spent a
stretch of time in a small Arizona desert town, evidently
drying out from two decades of furious traveling, performing, and socializing. Cut off from theater friends,
cocktail hours, and the official duties of the man of letters, he produced ninety pages of a new manuscript; the
book was to be called *Anthracite*, and it was his most ambitious fictional undertaking in terms of theme and design. Set in southern Illinois, Hoboken [New Jersey], St.
Kitts [in the Caribbean], and South America, the novel
dealt with the fortunes of a man falsely accused of mur-

der. Wilder—never a writer involved with tight plots—was interested less in the mystery and more in the large patterns of endurance in the protagonist's life. Kierkegaard's "man of faith" was Wilder's latest paradigm of human survival. Like *The Bridge*, this new narrative was involved with the purpose and coherence, if any, in our world. The book [which was retitled *The Eighth Day*] was designed to discover a new bridge in its protagonist's faith. And, like *The Skin of Our Teeth*, it was about reconstitution and evolution. Wilder earned little praise for this searching study of man's perdurability. . . .

Wilder was understandably disappointed by the generally cool reception of his strangely reflective novel, and changed styles and modes in his last work. *Theophilus North* is cast in an autobiographical mold and departs from the realistic manner of *The Eighth Day;* while the new book was fantastic, ironic, and charged by Wilder's cosmic sense, it was also somewhat bogged down by a combination of flat characterizations and nostalgia for the Newport of Wilder's youth. . . .

Wilder died in "the House the Bridge built" on December 7, 1975. While the honors piled up in the last decade, the creative satisfactions were meager when we measure his late work against the prose produced by [Ernest] Hemingway, [William] Faulkner, and [F. Scott] Fitzgerald in their last years. Nevertheless, Wilder did succeed in resisting the temptation to abandon his venturesome, outreaching idea of literature in favor of imitating his own successes, writing in one mode, or cultivating some familiar acreage. In his last novel he was overly caught up in his own fantasies: but the fact that he attempted yet another landscape and another style attests to his literary daring.

Tennessee Williams: Chronicler of Humanity's Darker Side

Alice Griffin

The South that Tennessee Williams (1911–1983) was born into and grew to cherish served as the setting for dozens of full-length dramas, one-act plays, and short stories. His success as a playwright came during his early thirties when *The Glass Menagerie* first played in Chicago and then opened to sold-out crowds on Broadway in 1945. Williams was a master of characterization, as evidenced by the multidimensional Blanche DuBois in *A Street Car Named Desire*. He did not hesitate to explore the darker side of human behavior and sexuality, subjects that often drew barbs from the critics. Some of his personal pains were played out in his dramas, especially the deep-seated grief and guilt he suffered after his sister, Rose, was given a lobotomy that sent her to a sanatorium for the rest of her life. Williams, too, endured the confines of a sanatorium in his efforts to cope with the depression and drug and alcohol abuse that

Alice Griffin, *Understanding Tennessee Williams*. Columbia: University of South Carolina Press, 1995. Copyright © 1995 by the University of South Carolina. Reproduced by permission.

followed the death of his lover, Frank Merlo.

In her book *Understanding Tennessee Williams*, author Alice Griffin shares the life and prolific career of this sensitive southerner who has left behind images of the downtrodden in the mid-twentieth-century South. Griffin is professor emerita and former director of graduate studies in English at Herbert H. Lehman College of the City University of New York. She is a theater critic for national and international publications and has written a number of books on playwrights and on Shakespeare's plays. She lives in Palm City, Florida, and London.

🐦 🐦 🐦

Thomas Lanier Williams was born on 26 March 1911, in the Episcopal rectory of Columbus, Mississippi, home of his maternal grandfather. His father, Cornelius Coffin Williams, was descended from "pioneer Tennessee stock," hence the writer's adopted first name. In 1918 the family moved to St. Louis, when his father, a traveling salesman for a shoe company, was promoted to the firm's headquarters there. Because of their Southern speech and manners, Tom and his older sister Rose, who had enjoyed a happy childhood, now became the butt of schoolmates' jokes. For the first time they realized they "were economically less fortunate than others." The family of five (his brother Dakin was born the next year) lived in a small apartment amid "ugly rows of apartment buildings the color of dried blood and mustard."

In junior high and high school Williams wrote poems and stories and at the age of sixteen won a prize from *Smart Set* magazine for his essay "Can a Good Wife Be a Good Sport?" He answered in the negative, assuming the role of a traveling salesman whose wife misbehaved in his absence. A year later his first short story was published in *Weird Tales*. His relations with his father were always difficult: "He was not a man capable of examining his behavior toward his family, or not capable of changing it. My mother devoted herself to us three kids and developed a hostility toward him, which he took out on me, the first male to replace him. He thought me, which I certainly was, a terrible sissy, and used to call me 'Miss Nancy' . . . because I wouldn't play baseball with the other boys and preferred girl playmates." At eleven Williams began a close childhood friendship, which ripened into love, with a neighbor, Hazel Kramer, "the greatest extrafamilial love of my life." He and Hazel were to part when his father insisted they not attend the same college.

Education Is Interrupted

Williams entered the University of Missouri in 1929, but in his third year, when he failed ROTC, his father refused to pay the tuition, and Williams returned home to work as a warehouse clerk for the International Shoe Company at sixty-five dollars a month. Working days and writing at night, he became exhausted and suffered a breakdown. He recuperated in Memphis at the home of his Dakin [maternal] grandparents, now retired from the ministry. Here he co-authored his first play, *Cairo! Shanghai! Bombay!* staged by an amateur group in 1935. He returned to St. Louis to finish college at Washington University but transferred to the University of Iowa in 1937 to study play writing and received his B.A. degree in English in 1938. While he was away, without his knowledge, his parents gave consent for his sister Rose to have a prefrontal lobotomy to cure her schizophrenia, which had grown steadily more acute. The operation was not a success; she remained institutionalized for the rest of her days, outliving her brother, whose guilt and whose love for his sister remained constant, as reflected in much of his writing, especially *The Glass Menagerie*.

After graduation Williams wandered about the country for a year, applied to the Work Projects Administration (WPA) writers' project in Chicago but was refused and traveled to New Orleans, where he had his first homosexual experience. In 1939, in an act that would change his life, he entered four of his one-act plays in a contest sponsored by the Group Theater in New York. The letter informing him of his hundred-dollar prize was signed by Harold Clurman, Theresa Helburn, and Molly Day Thacher (later Mrs. Elia Kazan). Audrey Wood became Williams's agent and secured for him a $1,000 grant from the Rockefeller Foundation.

With the money Williams went to New York to study advanced play writing with John Gassner and Erwin Piscator at the New School for Social Research. Gassner recommended that the Theater Guild produce Williams's play *Battle of Angels*, which opened in Boston at the end of 1940 with Miriam Hopkins in the leading role of Myra. Williams recalls, "The play was pretty far out for its time and included, among other tactical errors, a mixture of superreligiosity and hysterical sexuality coexisting in a central character. The critics and police censors seemed to regard this play as a theatrical counterpart of the bubonic plague surfacing in their city." The play quickly closed, and Williams began revising it in Key West, Florida. Seventeen years later it emerged as *Orpheus Descending*. In the military draft for World War II Williams received a 4F rating because of his bad health and supported himself during those years in various jobs, including waiter, teletype operator, cashier, and movie usher. He continued writing "not with any hope of making a living at it but because [he] found no other means of expressing things that seemed to demand expression": "There was never a moment when I did not find life to be immeasurably exciting to experience and to witness, however difficult it was to sustain."

A Rocky Road at MGM

But, having been a professional playwright, even though briefly, he was offered a six-month contract by MGM Studios at $250 a week to write a movie for [actress] Lana Turner. The studio turned down his film script and asked him to write one for Margaret O'Brien; he declined and proposed instead, as a new *Gone with the Wind*, a mammoth Southern epic, which was an early projection of *A Streetcar Named Desire*. MGM refused the proposal and also rejected his screenplay called *The Gentleman Caller*, which would become *The Glass Menagerie*. Then the studio dismissed Williams, but his pay continued until the contract expired, during which time he completed *The Glass Menagerie*. Once it opened on Broadway in March 1945, Williams's place in the American theater was assured.

In the next sixteen years all of the major plays would be produced, Williams would receive prizes, including Pulitzers, awards, honorary degrees, and invitations to membership in prestigious organizations. He published short stories, one-act plays, poetry, and a novel. Each of the major plays as well as one of the one-acts (*This Property Is Condemned*) was made into a motion picture.

In 1956 Williams's frank, outspoken film *Baby Doll* opened, to be blasted by the critics and condemned by New York's Cardinal Spellman. Twenty-seven of Williams's one-act plays have been published, including the two from which the film was derived, *Twenty-Seven Wagons Full of Cotton*, concerning a brutal Southern cotton-gin operator, his nubile wife, and a Latin visitor; and *The Unsatisfactory Supper*, portraying the trials of a birdlike spinster aunt who cooks for the household. Other outstanding one-acts written in the 1940s include: *The Purification*, a verse tragedy in the style of [Spanish dramatist Federico] García Lorca; *This Property Is Condemned*, a monologue by a pathetic Southern waif; *The Last of My Solid Gold Watches*, about a lonely traveling salesman at the end of his career; *Portrait of a Madonna*, about a faded Southern belle whose remembrance of lost love in times past ends with a trip to the sanitorium; *The Long Goodbye*, a young man's reverie about his mother and sister as movers empty their apartment; and *Lord Byron's Love Letters*, which became the libretto for an opera about an aging woman with romantic memories of an affair with Byron. These one-acts reveal Williams's skill at creating an artistic unity of characters, dialogue, and mood. The narrative line is slight, the exposition expertly handled, and the poetic monologues prefigure the long "arias" of the major plays, which premiered on Broadway from 1945 to 1961.

Surprised by Good Reviews

In 1958 the short play *Suddenly Last Summer* opened off Broadway; the good reviews surprised Williams, who confessed that he had expected to be run out of town on a rail; he regretted that the film version with Katharine Hepburn turned "a short morality play, in a lyrical style . . . into a sensationally successful film that the public thinks was a literal study of such things as cannibalism, madness, and sexual deviation." (An excellent television version directed by Richard Eyre appeared in 1992.) In 1960 Williams's second comedy, *Period of Adjustment*, opened to favorable reviews. It concerns two couples; the pair on their honeymoon, a sexually timid woman and an impotent man, arrive on Christmas eve to visit the man's former buddy, who is in the midst of a domestic imbroglio. Williams's humor is delightful, the farce fast-moving, and, even though minor Williams, the characterization, dialogue, and symbolism bear his unmistakable mark. The 1962 film with Jane Fonda and Tony Franciosa preserves most of the action as well as the original ending, a happy one, which therefore did not undergo the usual Hollywood transformation of Williams's conclusions.

Shaken by a Lover's Death

A fourteen-year intimacy with Frank Merlo began in 1948, and, when Merlo died of cancer in the 1960s, Williams endured depression, turned to alcohol and drugs, and spent three months in a mental institution. He refers to this period as his "Stoned Age." Although he continued to write every day, the plays from this period are minor ones. The least of them is interesting, for Williams never lost what he termed his "seventh sense" of theater, and three of the best ones, had they not been compared with his earlier works, might have been received more generously. They are *Small Craft Warnings, Out Cry (The Two-Character Play)*, and *Clothes for a Summer Hotel*.

The Milk Train Doesn't Stop Here Anymore was produced on Broadway in 1963, with Hermione Baddeley as the aged, temperamental Flora Goforth at whose Capri villa arrives a handsome young poet, Chris. His nickname is "Angel of Death" because his visits to ill older women always seem to culminate in their deaths. Although the action is erratic and the Kabuki-style scene changes disruptive, there is an elegiac mood created and sustained. The play concerns death and its acceptance, a motif introduced by the old poet Jonathan Coffin in *The Night of the Iguana*, now developed into a main theme in which the knell, or "boom," of the waves sounds continually. Some of the writing has the indelible Williams stamp, like Chris's speech in scene 5 about the two sleeping pets huddled together, whose "owner's house is never a sure protection, a reliable shelter. . . . We're all of us living in a house we're not used to . . . we try to—be—*pleasingly playful* . . . but—in our hearts, "we're all very frightened." The character of Flora is obviously autobiographical, as are central characters in succeeding plays.

It would seem that the more autobiographical Williams's later work became, the more he lost the fine artistic discipline and control that mark the major plays. After a very brief, unsuccessful run, *Milk Train* was revived with Tallulah Bankhead as Flora and made into a film in 1968 as *Boom!* with Elizabeth Taylor and Richard Burton, directed by Joseph Losey.

Painful Images

In 1966 Broadway saw the production of *Slapstick Tragedy*, a double bill of one-acts, including *The Gnädiges Fräulein* and *The Mutilated*. The latter concerns two women, both "mutilated," one by a mastectomy and the other by her wretched state, having just been released from jail. Each woman, despite berating the other, realizes their mutual dependency. The former, more weighty play, is satiric, expressionistic, farcical, and fantastic, with Margaret Leighton creating the title role of a once famous star, now a derelict, wearing her old finery, fighting the Cocaloony birds for fish, with which she pays for her lodging in the broken-down rooming house that is the setting. As the action progresses, she becomes increasingly mutilated by the Cocaloony, finally losing her eyes. Viewing the work as an allegory concerning Williams (the Fräulein), his competitors (the birds), and success (the fish), critic Harold Clurman declared it "an odd but effective mixture of gallows humor and Rabelaisian [referring to French writer François Rabelais] zest": "Though I was able to appreciate the style I could not bring myself to smile. I was too conscious that its author was in pain."

The Seven Descents of Myrtle (Kingdom of Earth) opened on Broadway in 1968 to unfavorable reviews. Reminiscent of [Eugene] O'Neill's *Desire Under the Elms*, but lacking its power and structure, the work concerns two brothers, Lot and Chicken. The effete, dying Lot marries Myrtle on a television show and brings her home, to prevent the earthy Chicken, who is illegitimate and half-black, from inheriting their farm. Lot succumbs, the floodwaters are rising, and the practical Myrtle realizes that her survival depends upon Chicken.

Small Craft Warnings was performed off-Broadway in 1972, an expanded version of an earlier short work, *Confessional*, in which each of the characters at various times leaves the action, advances downstage, and, spotlit, reveals, as if in a confession box, his or her innermost thoughts. The title refers literally to the marine warnings given small boats when rough weather is anticipated and, symbolically, to the collection of drifters and misfits who congregate nightly in a run-down beachfront bar. Another symbol of their plight is a mounted sailfish, once king of the sea but now worthless, dangling crazily as a ceiling decoration. The most lively customer is Leona, a tough, optimistic hairdresser. She has been sharing her mobile home with, but is about to dispossess, a stud who welcomes the advances of Violet, a weepy prostitute whose weakness contrasts with Leona's strength. When the actor playing Doc fell ill, Williams himself played the role of a has-been who performs illegal operations. The work is neither as optimistic as [William] Saroyan's *The Time of Your Life* nor as pessimistic as O'Neill's *The Iceman Cometh*, both of which it resembles. Good characterization, lively dialogue, and the presence of Williams (who from the stage participated in postperformance discussions) contributed to the deserved success of *Small Craft Warnings*. In 1975 Williams's autobiography *Memoirs* and his autobiographical novel *Moise and the World of Reason* both appeared.

Another Autobiographical Work

Another important Williams play, *Out Cry*, was presented on Broadway in 1973, with Michael York and Cara Duff-MacCormick as two actors, a brother and sister who find themselves locked in a theater, deserted by their touring company, with no scenery or audience; nevertheless, they proceed to enact their roles in the play-within-the-play. It concerns a tragedy in their own earlier lives in a Southern town. Poetic and free in its form, moving between the actors' lonely, fearful plight in the empty theater and their enactment of assigned roles in a scheduled play, the work was interpreted as autobiographical. In the *New York Times* of 2 May 1971 Williams describes the play's earlier version, *The Two-Character Play*, as "a tragedy with laughter": "It affirms nothing but gallantry in the face of defeat."

Two lesser plays opened in 1976 and 1977. *The Red Devil Battery Sign*, which played briefly in Boston, viewed international business, rather than society (as in earlier plays), as a destructive force. Intent on war, the Red Devil cartel will not be deterred by the weak idealists who oppose it, mambo musician King Del Ray (Anthony Quinn) and his Woman Downtown (Claire Bloom). In *Vieux Carré* on Broadway Sylvia Sidney played the domineering landlady Mrs. Wire in Williams's recreation of his early boardinghouse days in New Orleans. The inhabitants include a dying homosexual, two malnourished gentlewomen, a male hustler, and a once fashionable lady. The reviews of both plays were markedly unfavorable.

Another more appealing minor work, *A Lovely Sunday for Creve Coeur*, was presented on Broadway in 1979, set in St. Louis in the mid-1930s, with Shirley Knight as the delicate, Blanche-like high school teacher. Her practical German roommate, Bodey, steers Dorothea away from a hopeless liaison with the principal and into a day out with Bodey and her admiring, though stodgy, brother at the amusement park Creve Coeur.

The Fitzgeralds' Story

Clothes for a Summer Hotel, Williams's last full-length play to be staged on Broadway in his lifetime, opened in 1980 on his sixty-ninth birthday. The "summer hotel" is the mental institution in which Zelda Fitzgerald burned to death when the frame building was engulfed by fire and the confined patients could not flee. The central incident is a visit to his wife by F. Scott Fitzgerald, still wearing his Hollywood "summer clothes." Events move back and forth in time, detailing a brief affair of Zelda's, Scott's relationship with Ernest Hemingway, and the conflict between Zelda and Scott, whom she accuses of stifling her talent and stealing her life to create his successful novels. Some saw in this an analogy to Williams and his sister Rose. Although the structure may be sketchy and a knowledge of the Fitzgeralds' personal life is helpful, some of the dialogue is among Williams's best, and the mounting intensity highly dramatic, especially so because of Zelda's actual end.

Like Mark Antony's favoring god deserting him before the decisive battle, Williams's fortunes were against him on opening night. Although the leading roles were well played by Geraldine Page and Kenneth Haigh, the acoustical system at the Cort Theater developed a fault, causing a distraction, which seemed in part responsible for the unfavorable reviews from critics unable or unwilling to distinguish between the play and its production.

Alone in a hotel room in New York Williams died

three years later, having choked to death on the cap of an eye medicine bottle removed by and held in his teeth while leaning back to apply drops to his ever-ailing eyes. He had continued writing to the end, appending to his drafts the battle cry "En Avant" ["Forward"], struggling with bad health and his "blue devil," despairing over bad reviews. In 1970, in his prose poem read at a London poetry festival, Williams seems to anticipate his end: "not yet again, not so far . . . then very deep toe-curling stabs of a black-coated assassin's stiletto, that fierce opponent of your fierce will to continue, no, not that again, not so far, that long, long moment of air-starvation and anguish."

[Playwright] David Mamet's eulogy recounted Williams's impact on theater in the years of the major plays, and then, as "his life and view of life became less immediately accessible, our gratitude was changed to distant reverence for a man whom we felt obliged—if we were to continue in our happy feelings toward him—to consider already dead." The irony was apparent to Mamet, who observes that Americans are "a kind people living in a cruel country": "We don't know how to show our love. This was the subject of his plays, the greatest dramatic poetry in the American language. We thank him and we wish him, with love, the best we could have done and did not. We wish him what he wished us: the peace that we all are seeking."

Arthur Miller: Sympathizer with the Exploited

Jeffrey Meyers

Arthur Miller (1915–), who resides in Connecticut, is best known for his now-classic tale of the broken-spirited Willy Loman in *Death of a Salesman*, for which he was awarded the Pulitzer Prize in 1949. Miller's career spanned the second half of the twentieth century. He wrote numerous plays; a masterpiece autobiography, *Timebend*; and he has worked on films.

In the 1950s the New York City native was caught up in the quagmire of McCarthyism because of his leftist leanings, and he was questioned before the House Un-American Activities Committee. Afterward, he remained politically active, going abroad to fight for other writers' rights and serving as president of the writer's organization PEN International in the mideighties.

Miller's name will forever be linked with that of Marilyn Monroe, the psychologically fragile and tragic star who became his second wife in 1956 and starred in the film version of Miller's *The Misfits* in 1961. They divorced that year; she committed suicide in 1962.

In this excerpt from *Privileged Moments: Encounters with Writers*, Jeffrey Meyers shares not only the biographical de-

Jeffrey Meyers, *Privileged Moments: Encounters with Writers*. Madison: University of Wisconsin Press, 2000. Copyright © 2000 by the Board of Regents of the University of Wisconsin System. All rights reserved. Reproduced by permission.

tails of Miller's life but also glimpses into the thoughts and opinions of the celebrated playwright gained through several encounters and interviews during the early eighties. Meyers is the author of forty-three books, including biographies of Katherine Mansfield, Ernest Hemingway, D.H. Lawrence, Joseph Conrad, Edgar Allan Poe, F. Scott Fitzgerald, Edmund Wilson, Robert Frost, Humphrey Bogart, Gary Cooper, Errol and Sean Flynn, George Orwell, and Somerset Maugham. He lives in Berkeley, California.

🙐 🙐 🙐

In the 1970s I wrote two literary biographies: one on Katherine Mansfield, a short story writer from New Zealand who died early at the peak of her career; the other on Wyndham Lewis, an original novelist, great painter, and incurable outsider who died blind and neglected in 1957. As I began to consider a new subject, my biographer's antennae quivered at the thought of Arthur Miller. His opposition to the infamous House Un-American Activities Committee (HUAC) in the 1950s had earned him lasting political prestige. His plays were a staple of the American theater repertory, and he'd also written classic film scripts of his own work. Though his normal, commonsensical, intellectual life rarely made headlines, in the late 1950s he had been married to Marilyn Monroe, a conjunction that made heads spin at the time and now seemed the stuff of myth. I was full of respect for him, and curiosity as well.

In September 1980 I wrote to sound him out. . . .

My letter began our relationship. He asked me to send him my book on Mansfield, and read it attentively. "Though I usually distrust biographies," he wrote, "to the point of avoiding them whenever possible, yours I believed. . . . She is one of those tragic persons launched on a short trajectory, the self-consuming rocket." He invited me to visit him in Connecticut, and in June 1981 I made the first of nine visits, extending over the next seventeen years.

Arthur had bought this rustic house in 1956, a retreat from Manhattan and the theater, but close enough to New York to keep an eye on the city. Down a country lane, surrounded by forty acres of woods and meadows, it was set on a rise above a swimming pond. He came out to meet us, six feet tall, as straight-backed as a soldier, his white hair crowning his tanned bald head and his Jeffersonian face, familiar from many press photographs. He was as unpretentious as his house, a comfortable place with oriental rugs on the floor, colorful sofas, books overflowing the bookcases and scattered around the rooms. He had a carpentry workshop and separate studios for himself and his wife, the photographer Inge Morath [who died in January 2002]. . . .

The table was set for lunch out in the sunshine, and as we sat down Inge appeared, in a hurry to drive across the countryside to New Haven. She was taking a course in Chinese at Yale in preparation for their long trip— she to take photographs, he to direct *Death of a Salesman* in Beijing. . . .

Sitting across the table, Arthur looked strong and handsome. He'd injured his knee in a youthful football game and been rejected by the army in World War II. Recently, he'd fallen off a ladder and broken his ankle. (With it still in a cast he'd sailed up the Nile in Sadruddin Khan's yacht to see the Pharaonic monuments.) Just before a trip to South America, a tear in his retina almost blinded him. During a seven-hour emergency operation, performed the next day, the surgeon took the eyeball out of the socket and fastened a "buckle" around it to keep the tear from spreading. Though Arthur continued to be bothered by mist in his distant vision and had to rest his eyes in the afternoon, the operation saved his sight and gave him 20/20 vision with glasses. Apart from his ankle and his eyes, he was in remarkably good shape for a man of sixty-six. . . .

Profoundly Affected by the Depression

On my second visit we exchanged life stories, as people getting to know each other do, and Arthur talked more extensively about his past and present. His father, he said, had been barely literate but prosperous, his mother a high school graduate. They had lived comfortably in Manhattan, with servants and a chauffeur. When Arthur was fourteen his father lost everything in the Wall Street Crash, and never recovered his business or his wealth. He moved the family to Brooklyn and, cushioned by his remaining jewels and property, drifted slowly into poverty. This was the crucial experience of Arthur's life—the Depression, the ugly side of capitalism made manifest—which devastated the lives of his family and friends, but also inspired his poignant portrayal of Willy Loman. For the rest of his life he would sympathize with those who were exploited and then found themselves used up and discarded. . . .

Arthur married for the first time in 1940, Mary Slattery, a lapsed Catholic classmate at the University of Michigan who became a school psychologist. In 1956 they had a bitter separation, and he had not seen her for twenty years. Reflecting on the houses he had lived in (so important to a writer, whose home is his workshop), he told me that after his first success in the theater he had bought a Brooklyn Heights brownstone for $32,000 and lived there with his wife in the early 1950s. She had recently sold it for $650,000.

He bought the present Connecticut house, his second, when he married Marilyn Monroe. I pictured him in my mind's eye in all the photographs of the period, when the flashbulbs popped incessantly and Arthur Miller's face appeared next to Marilyn's in *Picture Post* and *Photoplay*. At forty-one, in the prime of his life and achievement, he was thinner then, tense and bespectacled. He didn't seem to go with the fluffy, artificial, lipsticked time bomb he had married. I thought of the photos of the group on location for *The Misfits* in the

Photographers followed Marilyn Monroe and Arthur Miller throughout their five-year marriage.

Nevada desert—Clark Gable, Montgomery Clift, Monroe, all doomed to die within the year—and Arthur, watching his screenplay develop as Monroe unraveled. Sitting in the lush quiet of the garden, I said surely this place must have made Marilyn happy. "Nothing could make Marilyn happy for very long," he flatly observed.

Futile Attempts to Help Marilyn Monroe

He spent so much on her treatment that he had to sell his literary manuscripts to the University of Texas. "Wasn't she rich, couldn't she pay for her own doctors?" I asked. He explained that, on the contrary, she was broke. She'd signed a seven-year contract with Fox that kept her on the same low salary after she became famous and earned them a fortune. Her photographer, Milton Greene, had formed a joint corporation with her, literally owning 49 percent of her. Arthur prevented him from getting majority control, but eventually Marilyn had to pay $100,000 to get rid of him.

From talk of Marilyn it was a short step to Norman Mailer, Arthur's bête noire, and to all the books about Marilyn "by trashy writers who never took her seriously." I then realized why Arthur was so sceptical about biography. He was particularly severe about his once close friend and collaborator Norman Rosten, who wrote the screenplay for *A View from the Bridge*, and called his book on Marilyn "superficial, vulgar, and self-justificatory." (Rosten had begun his career by winning a Yale Younger Poets prize, but he never fulfilled his promise.) Mailer's bizarre *Marilyn* (1975), a fantastical fiction masquerading as biography, claimed that Miller lived off her earnings, though Mailer could easily have found out that the reverse was true. Mailer invented witty and satiric remarks, directed against Miller, and put them into Marilyn's mouth. Arthur considered suing him, but finally decided that doing so would only help promote the book. At this point he was more disgusted than angry.

Arthur also thought the theory that the Kennedys had Marilyn murdered was absurd. She was probably sexually involved with them, but they were unlikely to have told her anything incriminating. In any case, she was loyal and they had no reason to kill her. As for Arthur's own relationship with Marilyn, which he did not talk about, I had the feeling that his happiness must have been brief, and that he'd spent most of his time trying to help this talented, wounded woman. Abused by so many men on her way to the top, she'd had several abortions and miscarriages. When they met she was suffering from depression and addicted to prescription drugs. The odds were against them, the decision to marry her an impulsive gamble for someone as self-controlled and self-respecting as Arthur Miller.

A Supportive Family

Inge Morath, by contrast, was and is eminently sane, strong, capable, and self-reliant. Always warm and welcoming—not the self-important dragon-guardian, like some literary wives—she is a cultured and sophisticated European intellectual, critical and alert. Her career and travels mesh with Arthur's, and she admires his work without lionizing him. . . .

Arthur has two children from his first marriage and one from his third. His son, Robert (born in 1947), who lived in California and worked in television, was a driving force in the [1996] movie of *The Crucible*. To raise money for this project, Arthur had sold in advance the rights to show the film on network television and HBO. Sixty directors, including Arthur Penn, had turned the film down because it had to be made in thirty days and none of them thought it could be done. Arthur's agent, Sam Cohn of International Creative

Management (ICM), reputedly the best in the business, had grave doubts they'd ever sell such a serious work in the age of "bang-bang" films. Finally, Robert asked if he could have the rights for six months. Within a few weeks, he sold it to Twentieth Century Fox and was made executive producer. John Briley, the scriptwriter of *Gandhi*, had done a screenplay. Arthur didn't like it and did one himself, writing half of the 140-page script in two weeks. He also went to Los Angeles to consult about the cast and director, and had wanted Kenneth Branagh for the leading role. *The Crucible* was Arthur's great money-maker. Even before the film came out, the play had sold eight million paperback copies in America and was Penguin's best-selling book.

Arthur's older daughter, Jane (born in 1944), was married to a sculptor and lived in New York. In the early 1990s she and her husband built a house near Arthur's on land he gave them. He was proud of Rebecca, his daughter with Inge, born in 1962. Beautiful and talented, educated at Choate and Yale, she learned three languages and graduated *cum laude*. Two of her paintings appeared on the covers of the English editions of Arthur's *Collected Plays* and she had several exhibitions in New York. She had a successful career as an actress, writer, and director, justifying Arthur's belief that an actor did not need formal training of the Lee Strasberg kind. . . .

Arthur's achievement came early in his life—though not quite so early as that of [F. Scott] Fitzgerald or [Ernest] Hemingway—and many theater critics in the 1980s seemed to assume that his work was somehow "over," that there are no second acts for American writers. But the constant revivals show that his early plays still resonate, still matter. His first great success in the theater, *All My Sons* (1947), became popular in both Israel and Egypt after the war of 1967. [Former Israeli] Prime Minister Shimon Peres, who sat next to Arthur at the opening, told him it could have been a contemporary Israeli play. Some of his countrymen were also profiteering from arms sales while others risked their lives in the air. To the Israeli audience the play was not mere entertainment and, as a mark of respect for the solemnity of the occasion, they did not applaud at the end. In Sweden, too, the portrayal of war guilt in the play touched a nerve. The Swedes were still troubled by the fact that they had allowed Nazi troops to pass through their country to invade Norway in World War II.

Arthur said he wrote the famous scene in *The Misfits* (1961) in which Roslyn flirtatiously plays with a ball and paddle in a bar, but Marilyn did some improvising and gave it final form in the movie. He liked and admired John Huston, the director. He described him as tall, gangling, lively, macho, and adventurous, an expert with horses—an important skill in the movie—both sensitive and brutal. A good writer, with discriminating taste, he was less interested in the finer points of acting than in the composition of the scene.

Jane's Blanket (1963), an oddity and perhaps Miller's rarest book, is his only children's story, named after his older daughter. The poet-anthologist Louis Untermeyer asked him, as well as other well-known writers, to contribute to a series of children's books. Arthur knew only one story and wrote it in an hour. Each foreign edition had its own distinctive artwork.

Whenever I went to visit him, and in occasional letters, Arthur also kept me up-to-date about the progress of his current work. In September 1982 he was casting and preparing to direct two one-act plays, *I Can't Remember Anything* and *Clara*, at the Long Wharf theater in New Haven. The plays concerned "the limits of reality." One portrayed a man who enters a boutique to buy a gift for a dying friend; the other was about a detective and a prostitute who knows the truth about a man wrongly convicted of murder. By the time I first met him, Arthur had given up on serious theater on Broadway, which had become completely commercial. He had no plans to bring his new plays to New York, but involved himself instead with provincial theater and London productions.

Miller's Own Story

The masterpiece of Arthur's late years is undoubtedly *Timebends* (1987). In a letter of April 1987, he said he was surprised and pleased with its reception: "I dreaded that its serpentine form . . . would put people off, but incredibly Book-of-the-Month has taken it," and it was translated into fifteen languages. Arthur had complained to me of the lack of historical background in the American reviews. My own review did not discuss the political side of Miller's life, but I noted the book's dominant themes: "the origins of creativity, the dangers of fame, the temptations of the flesh, the corruption of Hollywood, the commercialization of Broadway and the betrayal of American idealism." I explained that I was writing for William Buckley's conservative *National Review*—a magazine that would normally ignore the book—and that was not the place to discuss the communist witch-hunts of the 1950s.

The plot of the ironically titled film *Everybody Wins* (1990), originally called *Almost Everybody Wins*, was based on his one-act play *Some Kind of Love Story* (1984). In a New England mill town, a woman in her mid-thirties hires a private detective, an Irish ex-Chicago cop, to free a convicted murderer she knows to be innocent. The story explores the woman's multiple personalities which, for the detective, make all reality provisional. Though Arthur originally wanted Jack Nicholson for the leading role, the movie was made with Nick Nolte and Debra Winger. Though he's been in and out of the film business for years, Arthur remains psychologically detached from it. Movie stars who accumulate $50 million, he wryly observed, "become strange."

The Ride Down Mt. Morgan (1991) portrayed the confrontation of a wife and mistress around the hospital bed of a man who's had a car accident on an icy road. Arthur said it concerned the point at which an unpleasant but attractive man recognizes he's made a moral transgression. The play, like so many of his late works, is a mixture of the personal and subjective, the realistic and fantastic. He'd written more than a thousand pages of dialogue over a period of nine years before he knew where the play was going and could finish it—an interesting aside that tells us something of Miller's capacity to follow his urge, stick with an idea, and patiently develop it. The play was performed in London and Williamstown, and by the Public Theater in New York.

Arthur gladly signed all his books for me, and four of his inscriptions were illuminating. He wrote that *Situation Normal* (1944), his early book of military reportage, was "the first trigger pull." *In the Country* (1977), a charming book about Connecticut with photos by Inge, he called "This by now rare book and a favorite." He described the inspiration for *Everybody Wins* (1990) as "Things sometimes go whizzing off by themselves." And he linked the two settings of *The Archbishop's Ceiling* and *The American Clock*—an unnamed East European country (presumably Czechoslovakia) and the United States—by describing them as "two dangerously shaky, promising countries."

Lorraine Hansberry: A Youthful Voice for Civil Rights

Hugh Short

Lorraine Hansberry (1930–1965) never quite fit in. The young black playwright was raised in an upper-middle-class family in Chicago and was well educated. Her interests, however, were in Africa, black heritage, and the struggle of black Americans for civil rights. In her 1959 play, *A Raisin in the Sun*, she melded a dichotomy of influences and pressures from the black and white worlds into a black family struggling to attain its American dream. The play was the first drama by a black woman to be produced on Broadway. It was critically acclaimed, and at the age of twenty-nine, Hansberry won the New York Drama Critics Circle Award, becoming the youngest American, the first woman, and the first black to take the honor. Sadly, she was stricken with cancer and died at the age of thirty-four; her second play, *The Sign in Sidney Brustein's Window*, closed that day.

This biographical sketch by Hugh Short recounts Hansberry's brief but profound career and the social injustices she chose to expose. Short is department chair and associate professor in the English department at Iona College in

Hugh Short, updated by Katherine Lederer, "Lorraine Hansberry," *Critical Survey of Drama*, edited by Carl Rollyson. Pasadena, CA: Salem Press, 2003. Copyright © 2003 by Salem Press, Inc. Reproduced by permission.

New Rochelle, New York. His teaching interests include twentieth-century American literature, composition, and rhetoric. He has published articles on drama and dramatists and is currently writing a piece on novelist William Faulkner.

🐞 🐞 🐞

Lorraine Hansberry's career was very brief, only two of her plays being produced in her lifetime, yet she recorded some very impressive theatrical achievements. She was only twenty-nine when *A Raisin in the Sun* appeared on Broadway, and its great success earned for her recognition that continues to this day. When *A Raisin in the Sun* was voted best play of the year by the New York Drama Critics Circle, she became the first black person as well as the youngest person to win the award. In 1973, a musical adapted from *A Raisin in the Sun*, entitled *Raisin* (with libretto by [her ex-husband Robert] Nemiroff), won a Tony Award as best musical of the year (1974). . . . Though her later work has received far less recognition than her first play, *A Raisin in the Sun* continues to enjoy a broad popularity.

Lorraine Vivian Hansberry was born on May 19, 1930, in the South Side of Chicago, the black section of the city. Her parents, Carl and Mamie Hansberry, were well-off. Her father was a United States deputy marshal for a time and then opened a successful real estate business in Chicago. Despite her family's affluence, they were forced by local covenants to live in the poor South Side. When Hansberry was eight years old, her father decided to test the legality of those covenants by buying a home in a white section of the city. Hansberry later recalled one incident that occurred shortly after the family's move to a white neighborhood: A mob gathered outside their home, and a brick, thrown through a window, barely missed her before embedding itself in a wall.

In order to stay in the house, to which he was not given clear title, Carl Hansberry instituted a civil rights suit against such restrictive covenants. When he lost in Illinois courts, he and the National Association for the Advancement of Colored People (NAACP) carried an appeal to the United States Supreme Court, which, on November 12, 1940, reversed the ruling of the Illinois supreme court and declared the local covenants illegal. Thus, Lorraine had a consciousness of the need to struggle for civil rights from a very young age. Her father, despite his legal victory, grew increasingly pessimistic about the prospects for change in the racial situation, and he finally decided to leave the country and retire in Mexico City. He had a stroke during a visit to Mexico, however, and died in 1945.

African Influence

Hansberry's uncle, William Leo Hansberry, was also an important influence on her. A scholar of African history who taught at Howard University, his pupils included Nnamdi Azikewe, the first president of Nigeria, and Kwame Nkrumah [who was a leader] of Ghana [and a proponent for a United Africa]. Indeed, William Leo Hansberry was such a significant figure in African studies that in 1963, the University of Nigeria named its College of African Studies at Nsakka after him. While Lorraine was growing up, she was frequently exposed to the perspectives of young African students who were invited to family dinners, and this exposure helped to shape many of the attitudes later found in her plays.

Lorraine, the youngest of four children, was encouraged to excel and was expected to succeed. After attending Englewood High School, she enrolled in the

University of Wisconsin as a journalism student. She did not fare very well at the university, however, and felt restricted by the many requirements of the school. After two years, she left Wisconsin and enrolled in the New School for Social Research in New York, where she was permitted greater leeway in choosing courses.

Once in New York, Hansberry began writing for several periodicals, including *Freedom*, [actor and singer] Paul Robeson's monthly magazine. She quickly became a reporter and then an associate editor of the magazine. In New York, she met Robert Nemiroff, then a student at New York University, and they were married in June of 1953. By this time, Hansberry had decided to be a writer, and although the bulk of her energies went into writing, she did hold a variety of jobs during the next few years. When Nemiroff acquired a good position with music publisher Phil Rose, she quit working and began writing full-time.

Brief Struggle, Huge Success

Hansberry's first completed work was *A Raisin in the Sun*, which, after an initial struggle for financial backing, opened on Broadway at the Ethel Barrymore Theatre on March 11, 1959. The play, starring Sidney Poitier, Ruby Dee, Louis Gossett, Jr., and Claudia Mc-Neil, was an enormous success, running for 530 performances, and in May, winning the New York Drama Critics Circle Award.

Soon thereafter, Hansberry and Nemiroff moved from their apartment in Greenwich Village to a home in Croton, New York, in order for Hansberry to have more privacy for her work. At the same time, her success made her a public figure, and she used her newfound fame to champion the causes of civil rights and African independence. She made important speeches in a variety of places and once confronted then Attorney

General Robert Kennedy on the issue of civil rights.

It was not until 1964 that Hansberry produced another play, *The Sign in Sidney Brustein's Window*, and by that time she was seriously ill. The play opened at the Longacre Theatre on October 15, 1964, to generally good but unenthusiastic reviews, and Nemiroff had to struggle to keep it open, a number of times placing advertisements in newspapers asking for support, accepting financial support from friends and associates, and once accepting the proceeds from a spontaneous collection taken up by the audience when it was announced that without additional funds, the play would have to close. On this uncertain financial basis, production of the play continued from week to week.

A Victim of Cancer

Hansberry's life continued in much the same way. While the play struggled, she was in a hospital bed dying of cancer. She once lapsed into a coma and was not expected to recover, but for a brief time she did rally, recovering all of her faculties. Her strength gave out, however, and on January 12, 1965, she died. That night, the Longacre Theatre closed its doors in mourning, and *The Sign in Sidney Brustein's Window* closed after 101 performances.

Realistic Style

Lorraine Hansberry claimed [Irish playwright] Sean O'Casey as one of the earliest and strongest influences on her work and cited his realistic portrayal of character as the source of strength in his plays. In *To Be Young, Gifted, and Black*, she praised O'Casey for describing

> the human personality in its totality. O'Casey never fools you about the Irish . . . the Irish drunkard, the Irish braggart, the Irish liar . . . and the genuine heroism which must naturally emerge when you tell the

truth about people. This . . . is the height of artistic perception . . . because when you believe people so completely . . . then you also believe them in their moments of heroic assertion: you don't doubt them.

In her three most significant plays, *A Raisin in the Sun*, *The Sign in Sidney Brustein's Window*, and *Les Blancs*, one can see Hansberry's devotion to the principles that she valued in O'Casey. First, she espoused realistic drama; second, she believed that the ordinary individual has a capacity for heroism; and finally, she believed that drama should reveal to the audience its own humanity and its own capacity for heroism.

Hansberry claimed that her work was realistic rather than naturalistic, explaining that

naturalism tends to take the world as it is and say: this is what it is . . . it is "true" because we see it every day in life . . . you simply photograph the garbage can. But in realism . . . the artist . . . imposes . . . not only what *is* but what is *possible* . . . because that is part of reality too.

For Hansberry, then, realism involved more than a photographic faithfulness to the real world. She sought to deliver a universal message but realized that "in order to create the universal you must pay very great attention to the specific. Universality . . . emerges from truthful identity of what is." This concern for realism was present from the very beginning of Hansberry's career and persists in her work, though she did occasionally depart from it in small ways, such as in the symbolic rather than literal presence of "The Woman" in *Les Blancs*, that character symbolizing the spirit of liberty and freedom that lives inside humanity.

Ordinary Heroes

Essential to Hansberry's vision of reality was the belief that the average person has within him or her the capacity for heroism. Hansberry believed that each human being is not only "dramatically interesting" but also a "creature of stature," and this is one of the most compelling features of her drama. Like O'Casey, Hansberry paints a full picture of each character, complete with flaws and weaknesses, yet she does not permit these flaws to hide the characters' "stature." Perhaps she expressed this idea best in *A Raisin in the Sun*, when Lena Younger berates her daughter Beneatha for condemning her brother, Walter Lee. Lena says, "When you start measuring somebody, measure him right, child, measure him right. Make sure you done taken into account what hills and valleys he come through before he got to wherever he is." For Hansberry, each character's life is marked by suffering, struggle, and weakness, yet in each case, the final word has not been written. Just as Beneatha's brother can rise from his degradation, just as Sidney (in *The Sign in Sidney Brustein's Window*) can overcome his ennui, so each of her characters possesses not only a story already written but also possibilities for growth, accomplishment, and heroism. Hansberry permits no stereotypes in her drama, opting instead for characters that present a mixture of positive and negative forces.

Hope for Humanity

Hansberry's realistic style and her stress on the possibilities for heroism within each of her characters have everything to do with the purpose that she saw in drama. As [writer] James Baldwin observed, Hansberry made no bones about asserting that art has a purpose, that it contained "the energy that could change things." In *A Raisin in the Sun*, Hansberry describes a poor black family living in Chicago's South Side, her own childhood home, and through her realistic portrayal of their financial, emotional, and racial struggles, as well as in her depiction of their ability to prevail, she offers her audience a model of hope and perseverance and shows the commonality of human aspirations, regardless of color. In *The Sign in Sidney Brustein's Window*, she takes as her subject the disillusioned liberal Sidney Brustein, who has lost faith in the possibility of creating a better world. After all of his disillusionment, he realizes that despair is not an answer, that the only answer is hope despite all odds and logic, that change depends on his commitment to it. So too, in *Les Blancs*, Hansberry gives her audience a character, Tshembe Matoseh, who has a comfortable, pleasant, secure life and who seeks to avoid commitment to the cause of African independence, though he believes in the justness of that cause. He learns that change comes about only through commitment, and that such commitment often means the abandonment of personal comfort on behalf of something larger.

Appendix of Documents

Document 1: Aristophanes Mocks Euripides

Aristophanes often delivered his witty and coarse humor at the expense of others. In Thesmophoriazusae *(Women's Festival), produced at the Great Dionysia in Athens in 411* B.C., *Aristophanes took aim at his favorite target, tragic poet Euripides, among others. In the play, the character Euripides finds himself in a potentially deadly predicament: The women of Athens plan to meet at the Temple of Demeter to determine Euripides' punishment for degrading the female sex in his tragedies. Fearing he will be condemned to death unless someone is there to defend him, Euripides tries to convince his friend, poet Agathon (portrayed as an effeminate youth), to dress as a woman and infiltrate the assembly.*

EURIPIDES (*to* AGATHON)
But listen to the cause that brings me here.

AGATHON
Say on.

EURIPIDES
Agathon, wise is he who can compress many thoughts into few words. Struck by a most cruel misfortune, I come to you as a suppliant.

AGATHON
What are you asking?

EURIPIDES
The women purpose killing me to-day during the Thesmophoria [festival for women only], because I have dared to speak ill of them.

AGATHON
And what can I do for you in the matter?

EURIPIDES

Everything. Mingle secretly with the women by making yourself pass as one of themselves; then do you plead my cause with your own lips, and I am saved. You, and you alone, are capable of speaking of me worthily.

AGATHON

But why not go and defend yourself?

EURIPIDES

Impossible. First of all, I am known; further, I have white hair and a long beard; whereas you, you are good-looking, charming, and are close-shaven; you are fair, delicate, and have a woman's voice.

AGATHON

Euripides!

EURIPIDES

Well?

AGATHON

Have you not said in one of your pieces, "You love to see the light, and don't you believe your father loves it too?"

EURIPIDES

Yes.

AGATHON

Then never you think I am going to expose myself in your stead; it would be madness. It's up to you to submit to the fate that overtakes you; one must not try to trick misfortune, but resign oneself to it with good grace.

Whitney J. Oates and Eugene O'Neill Jr., eds. *The Complete Greek Drama: All the Extant Tragedies of Aeschylus, Sophocles, and Euripides, and the Comedies of Aristophanes and Menander, in a Variety of Translations*, vol. 2. New York: Random House, 1938, pp. 875–76.

Document 2: Coroner's Report on Christopher Marlowe's Death

Christopher Marlowe's life and flourishing career as a dramatist were cut short when in 1593 he was stabbed to death at the age of twenty-nine. Because the playwright was suspected of performing surreptitious work as a government agent or spy, some scholars argue that his death was really an assassination. The coroner's report, however, tells a different story, reporting that Ingram Frizer [Ingram ffrysar) killed Marlowe in self-defense during a heated quarrel over their supper bill.

Kent./ Inquisition indented taken at Detford Strand in the aforesaid County of Kent within the verge on the first day of June in the year of the reign of Elizabeth by the grace of God of England France & Ireland Queen defender of the faith &c thirty-fifth, in the presence of William Danby, Gentleman, Coroner of the household of our said lady the Queen, upon view of the body of Christopher Morley [Marlowe], there lying dead & slain, upon oath of Nicholas Draper, Gentleman, Wolstan Randall, gentleman, William Curry, Adrian Walker, John Barber, Robert Baldwyn, Giles ffeld, George Halfepenny, Henry Awger, James Batt, Henry Bendyn, Thomas Batt senior, John Baldwyn, Alexander Burrage, Edmund Goodcheepe, & Henry Dabyns, Who say [upon] their oath that when a certain Ingram ffrysar, late of London, Gentleman, and the aforesaid Christopher Morley and one Nicholas Skeres, late of London, Gentleman, and Robert Poley of London aforesaid, Gentleman, on the thirtieth day of May in the thirty-fifth year above named, at Detford Strand aforesaid in the said County of Kent within the verge, about the tenth hour before noon of the same day, met together in a room in the house of a certain Eleanor Bull, widow; & there passed the time together & dined & after dinner were in quiet sort together there & walked in the garden belonging to the said house until the sixth hour after noon of the same day & then returned from the said garden to the room aforesaid & there together and in company supped; & after supper the said Ingram & Christopher Morley were in speech & uttered one to the other divers malicious words for the reason that they could not be at one nor agree about the payment of the sum of pence, that is, *le recknynge*, there; & the said Christopher Morley then lying upon a bed in the room where they supped, & moved with anger against the said Ingram ffrysar upon the words as aforesaid spoken between them, And the said Ingram then & there sitting in the room aforesaid with his back towards the bed where the said Christopher Morley was then lying, sitting near the bed, that is, *nere the bed*, & with the front part of his body towards the table & the aforesaid Nicholas Skeres & Robert Poley sitting on either side of the said Ingram in such a manner that the same Ingram ffrysar in no wise could take flight: it so befell that the said Christopher Morley on a sudden & of his malice towards the said Ingram aforethought, then & there maliciously drew the dagger of the said Ingram which was at his back, and with the same dagger the said Christopher Morley then & there maliciously gave the aforesaid Ingram two wounds on his head of the length of two inches & of the depth of a quarter of an inch; whereupon the said Ingram, in fear of being slain, & sitting in the manner aforesaid between the said Nicholas Skeres & Robert Poley so that he could not in any wise get away, in his own defence & for the saving of his life, then & there struggled with the said Christopher Morley to get back from him his dagger aforesaid; in which affray the same Ingram could not get away from the said Christopher Morley; and so it befell in that affray that the said Ingram, in defence of his life, with the dagger aforesaid of the value of 12d. gave the said Christopher then & there a mortal wound over his right eye of the depth of two inches & of the width of one inch; of which mortal wound the aforesaid Christopher Morley then & there instantly died; And so the Jurors aforesaid say upon their oath that the said Ingram killed & slew Christopher Morley aforesaid on the thirtieth day of May in the thirty-fifth year named above at Detford Strand aforesaid within the verge in the room aforesaid within the verge in the manner and form aforesaid in the defence and saving of his own life, against the peace of our said lady the Queen, her now crown & dignity; And further the said Jurors say upon their oath that the said Ingram after the slaying aforesaid perpetrated & done by him in the manner & form aforesaid neither fled nor withdrew himself; But what goods or chattels, lands or tenements the said Ingram had at the time of the slaying aforesaid, done & perpetrated by him in the manner and form aforesaid, the said Jurors are totally ignorant. In witness of which thing the said Coroner as well as the Jurors aforesaid to this Inquisition have interchangeably set their seals.

Given the day & year above named &c

by William Danby
Coroner.

J. Leslie Hotson, *The Death of Christopher Marlowe*. London: Nonesuch Press, 1925, pp. 31–34.

Document 3: The Quotable Shakespeare

William Shakespeare's contribution to the English language is un-precedented, and speakers of the language continually quote him—whether consciously or unconsciously—in everyday speech. In a lecture on Shakespeare Quotation, *delivered in the early 1900s before the Adelaide University Shakespeare Society in South Australia, the Hon. Sir Josiah Symon demonstrated how common Shakespeare's words and phrases have become in modern English.*

How constantly in our very commonest and every-day talk we are indebted to Shakespeare for pointed terms and turns of speech. How pretty it is to think of the cook or the kitchen maid as "the kitchen vestal," and yet it is not unheard of that she should "sauce her mistress" with "bitter words" "Base is the slave that pays" not unnaturally introduces to the creditor "I'll see thee hanged first," although "He knows too much," or, in a still more incisive form, "A trick worth two of that." "The curled darlings" and the "great oneyers" of modern society were so named by Shakespeare, who taught us to say "Second to none," "Come warble," "Play the fool," "What the dickens," "Have the start of me," "Dance attendance," "Harp not on that string,", "All's one for that." "Too, too" is Shakespeare's, and outlives the late fashionable slang, "Quite too, too"; and so is "To take a nap," "Good old man," "Bag and baggage," "Holiday humour," "An ill-favoured thing, but mine own," "Truth will out," "A burning shame," and "Too old to learn." Words in a familiar or even slang acceptation are as we have received them from Shakespeare—"He parted well and paid his score," "'Twere good you knocked him,"

"Hammering at" a subject, or "Hammer it out," "Peppered" (in the sense of being plentifully shot at); "Trudge" and "Pack," and so "Care killed a cat," "Fobbed off," "Water in a sieve," "Eat your word," "They that touch pitch will be defiled," "The seamy side," "The pity of it." "Eaten up with passion," "Othello's occupation gone," "Free and open nature," "Nothing if not critical," "Every mother's son," "Led by the nose," "Food for powder," "The game's afoot," "Clerkly done," "Quaintly writ," "Prophetic soul," and "Lards the lean earth."

These, too, are only examples. It would be interesting to compile a complete list.

Josiah Symon, *Shakespeare the Englishman.* New York: Haskell House, 1971, pp. 197–99.

Document 4: Ben Jonson Remembers Shakespeare

Ben Jonson probably met fellow dramatist Shakespeare when the latter acted in Jonson's Every Man in His Humour *in London in 1598. Jonson's respect and admiration for Shakespeare and his work are evident in this excerpt from Jonson's poetic preface to the* First Folio, *the first edition of Shakespeare's collected works, published in 1623.*

To the memory of my beloved,
The Author
MR. WILLIAM SHAKESPEARE:
AND
what he hath left us.

> To draw no envy (Shakespeare) on thy name,
> Am I thus ample to thy Booke, and Fame;
> While I confesse thy writings to be such,
> As neither Man, nor Muse, can praise too much.
> 'Tis true, and all men's suffrage. But these wayes
> Were not the paths I meant unto thy praise;
> For seeliest Ignorance on these may light,
> Which, when it sounds at best, but eccho's right;
> Or blinde Affection, which doth ne're advance

The truth, but gropes, and urgeth all by chance;
Or crafty Malice, might pretend this praise,
And thine to ruine, where it seem'd to raise.
These are, as some infamous Baud, or Whore,
Should praise a Matron. What could hurt her more?
But thou art proofe against them, and indeed
Above th' ill fortune of them, or the need.
I, therefore will begin. Soule of the Age!
The applause! delight! the wonder of our Stage!
. . . a good Poet's made, as well as borne.
And such wert thou. Looke how the fathers face
Lives in his issue, even so, the race
Of Shakespeares minde, and manners brightly shines
In his well toned, and true-filed lines:
In each of which, he seemes to shake a Lance,
As brandish't at the eyes of Ignorance.
Sweet swan of Avon! what a fight it were
To see thee in our waters yet appeare,
And make those flights upon the bankes of Thames,
That so did take Eliza, and our James!
But stay, I see thee in the Hemisphere
Advanc'd, and made a Constellation there!
Shine forth, thou Starre of Poets, and with rage,
Or influence, chide, or cheere the drooping Stage;
Which, since thy flight fro' hence, hath mourn'd like night,
And despaires day, but for thy Volumes light.

BEN JONSON.

Alfred Harbage, ed., *The Complete Pelican Shakespeare*. Baltimore: Penguin Books, 1969, pp. xix–xx.

Document 5: Napoléon Interviews Goethe

German-born Johann Wolfgang von Goethe (1749–1832) left a tremendous mark on German literature with his novel The Sorrows of Young Werther *and his poetic drama* Faust. *Napoléon Bonaparte, emperor of France, admired the man and his work. On October 2, 1808, Goethe was received by Napoléon, who had as-*

sembled the Congress of Erfurt (France), during which the Franco-Russian alliance was renewed. Present at the exchange between Goethe and Napoléon was French statesman Charles Maurice de Talleyrand-Périgord, Prince de Bénévent, who wrote an account of the meeting, from which this excerpt is taken, and later published it in his memoirs.

"Monsieur Goethe," [Napoléon] said to him on seeing him, "I am delighted to see you."

"Sire, I see that when your Majesty travels, you do not neglect to notice even the most insignificant persons."

"I know you are Germany's first dramatic poet."

"Sire, you wrong our country; we are under the impression we have our great men. [Friedrich] Schiller, [Gotthold] Lessing, and [Christophe Martin] Wieland are surely known to your Majesty.". . .

"While you are here, you must go every night to our plays. It will not do you any harm to see good French tragedies" [Napoléon said].

"I'll go willingly. I must confess to your Majesty that it was my intention, for I have translated, or rather imitated, some French pieces."

"Which ones?"

"*Mahomet* and *Tancred*" [by French author, dramatist, and philosopher Voltaire].

"I shall ask [Auguste Laurent, Comte de] Rémusat [chamberlain to Napoléon] if he has any actors here to play them. I should be very glad for you to see them represented in our language. You are not as strict as we are in theatrical rules."

"Sire, unity with us is not so essential."

"How do you find our sojourn here?"

"Very brilliant, sire, and I hope it will be useful to our country."

"Are your people happy?"

"They hope to be so soon."

"Monsieur Goethe, you ought to remain with us during the whole of our stay and write your impressions of the grand sight we are offering."

"Ah! sire, it would require the pen of some great writer of

antiquity to undertake such a task." . . .

"Monsieur Goethe, come to-night to *Iphigenia* [Jean Racine's tragedy]. It is a good piece. It is not, however, one of my favourites, but the French think a good deal of it. You will see in my pit a great number of sovereigns. Do you know the Prince Primate [Karl Theodor von Dalberg]?"

"Yes, sire; almost intimately. He is very clever, very well informed, and very generous."

"Well, you will see him, to-night, fast asleep on the shoulder of the King of Württemberg [Frederick I]. Have you already seen the Czar [Alexander I of Russia]?"

"No, sire, never; but I hope to be introduced to him."

"He speaks your language; should you write anything on the Erfurt interview, you must dedicate it to him."

"Sire, it is not my habit to do so. When I first commenced to write, I made it a principle never to dedicate anything to any one, in order that I should never repent it."

"The great writers of [the king of France] Louis the Fourteenth's time were not of your opinion."

"But your Majesty cannot be sure they never repented doing what they did."

"What has become of that scoundrel, [August von] Kotzebue?" [Political pamphleteer and author of comedies]

"Sire, they say he is in Siberia and that his Majesty will solicit his pardon from the Czar."

"But he is not the man for me."

"Sire, he has been very unfortunate, and is a man of great talent."

"Good-bye, Monsieur Goethe."

Berthold Biermann, ed., *Goethe's World as Seen in Letters and Memoirs.* New York: New Directions Books, 1949, pp. 287–88.

Document 6: George Bernard Shaw Explains Ibsenism: Realism vs. Idealism

Henrik Ibsen's progress as a playwright can be marked by his changes in style and content. He opted to turn from romantic verse to realistic prose and is best known for his plays that rebelled against the accepted social ideals of the 1800s. In 1913, George Bernard Shaw, author, dramatist, and critic, published The Quintessence of Ibsenism, *which explained Ibsen's realistic, or anti-idealistic, way of thinking and how the Norwegian playwright conveyed his philosophies in his dramas. In this excerpt, Shaw contrasts the realist and idealist.*

The realist at last loses patience with ideals altogether, and sees in them only something to blind us, something to numb us, something to murder self in us, something whereby, instead of resisting death, we can disarm it by committing suicide. The idealist, who has taken refuge with the ideals because he hates himself and is ashamed of himself, thinks that all this is so much the better. The realist, who has come to have a deep respect for himself and faith in the validity of his own will, thinks it so much the worse. To the one, human nature, naturally corrupt, is held back from ruinous excesses only by self-denying conformity to the ideals. To the other these ideals are only swaddling clothes which man has outgrown, and which insufferably impede his movements. No wonder the two cannot agree. The idealist says, "Realism means egotism; and egotism means depravity." The realist declares that when a man abnegates the will to live and be free in a world of the living and free, seeking only to conform to ideals for the sake of being, not himself, but "a good man," then he is morally dead and rotten, and must be left unheeded to abide his resurrection, if that by good luck arrive before his bodily death. Unfortunately, this is the sort of speech that nobody but a realist understands.

George Bernard Shaw, *The Quintessence of Ibsenism*. New York: Hill and Wang, 1913, pp. 44–45.

Document 7: Oscar Wilde Writes of His Humiliation

The flamboyant Oscar Wilde was at the height of his career as a playwright when in 1895 his life took a 180-degree turn. That year he was convicted and imprisoned for homosexual offenses, and his reputation became one of notoriety rather than of celebrity. In 1897, while incarcerated at Reading Gaol, he composed a lengthy

and emotional letter to his former lover Lord Alfred "Bosie"
Douglas, in which he recounted the humiliating experience of be-
ing transported to prison in convict garb. Extracts from the letter
were first published as De Profundis *in 1905, and a more com-*
plete version of the letter—littered with errors—was published in
1949. This excerpt is from an accurate version.

To Lord Alfred Douglas
MS. B.M.

[January–March 1897]   *H.M. Prison, Reading*
Dear Bosie, After long and fruitless waiting I have determined to write to you myself, as much for your sake as for
mine, as I would not like to think that I had passed through
two long years of imprisonment without ever having received a single line from you, or any news or message even,
except such as gave me pain. . . .

Everything about my tragedy has been hideous, mean, re-
pellent, lacking in style. Our very dress makes us grotesques.
We are the zanies of sorrow. We are clowns whose hearts are
broken. We are specially designed to appeal to the sense of
humour. On November 13th 1895 I was brought down here
from London. From two o'clock till half-past two on that
day I had to stand on the centre platform of Clapham Junc-
tion in convict dress and handcuffed, for the world to look
at. I had been taken out of the Hospital Ward without a
moment's notice being given to me. Of all possible objects I
was the most grotesque. When people saw me they laughed.
Each train as it came up swelled the audience. Nothing
could exceed their amusement. That was of course before
they knew who I was. As soon as they had been informed,
they laughed still more. For half an hour I stood there in the
grey November rain surrounded by a jeering mob. For a
year after that was done to me I wept every day at the same
hour and for the same space of time. That is not such a tragic
thing as possibly it sounds to you. To those who are in
prison, tears are a part of every day's experience. A day in
prison on which one does not weep is a day on which one's
heart is hard, not a day on which one's heart is happy.

Well, now I am really beginning to feel more regret for

the people who laughed than for myself. Of course when they saw me I was not on my pedestal. I was in the pillory. But it is a very unimaginative nature that only cares for people on their pedestals. A pedestal may be a very unreal thing. A pillory is a terrific reality. They should have known also how to interpret sorrow better. I have said that behind Sorrow there is always Sorrow. It were still wiser to say that behind sorrow there is always a soul. And to mock at a soul in pain is a dreadful thing. Unbeautiful are their lives who do it. In the strangely simple economy of the world people only get what they give, and to those who have not enough imagination to penetrate the mere outward of things and feel pity, what pity can be given save that of scorn? . . .

Your affectionate friend,
Oscar Wilde

Rupert Hart-Davis, ed., *The Letters of Oscar Wilde*. New York: Harcourt, Brace & World, 1962, pp. 490–91.

Document 8: Anton Chekhov Recalls an Execution on Sakhalin Island

In 1890 when Russian writer and physician Anton Chekhov left his writing projects, his medical practice, and his family and friends to make the long, rigorous journey to the penal colony on Sakhalin Island in Siberia, Russia, he said he was going "for scientific and literary purposes." While there he spent three months taking a census of the population, observing the prisoners, and recording the degrading conditions. In 1895 he published his completed findings, from which this excerpt is taken, but the treatise did little to incite change.

Eleven men were sentenced to death for the murder of some Ainus in the Korsakov district. None of the officers and officials slept on the night before the execution; they visited each other and drank tea. There was a general feeling of exhaustion; nobody found a comfortable place to rest in. Two of the condemned men poisoned themselves with wolfsbane—a tremendous embarrassment to the military officials responsible for the execution of the sentences. The district commander heard a tumult during the night and was then informed that the two prisoners had poisoned themselves. When everyone had gathered around the scaffold just before the execution, the district commander found himself saying to the officer in charge:

"Eleven were sentenced to death, but I see only nine here. Where are the other two?"

Instead of replying in the same official manner, the officer in charge said in a low, nervous voice:

"Why don't you hang me! Hang me. . . ."

It was an early October morning, gray, cold and dark. The faces of the prisoners were yellow with fear and their hair was waving lightly. An official read out the death sentence, trembling with nervousness and stuttering because he could not see well. The priest, dressed in black vestments, presented the Cross for all nine to kiss, and then turned to the district commander, whispering:

"For God's sake, let me go, I can't. . . ."

The procedure is a long one. Each man must be dressed in a shroud and led to the scaffold. When they finally hanged the nine men, there was "an entire bouquet" hanging in the air—these were the words of the district commander as he described the execution to me. When the bodies were lifted down the doctors found that one was still alive.

This incident had a peculiar significance. Everyone in the prison, all those who knew the innermost secrets of the crimes committed by the inmates, the hangman and his assistants—all of them knew he was alive because he was innocent of the crime for which he was being hanged.

"They hanged him a second time," the district commander concluded his story. "Later I could not sleep for a whole month."

Anton Chekhov, *The Island: A Journey to Sakhalin*, trans. Luba and Michael Terpak. New York: Washington Square Press, 1967, pp. 334–35.

Document 9: Eugene O'Neill at His Father's Deathbed

Eugene O'Neill was exposed to the theater from the beginning of his life. The Irish American family was often on the road, moving from hotel room to hotel room. James Sr. was a heavy drinker, and sons Eugene and Jamie became alcoholics too. But regardless of his father's vices, Eugene described his father as a "good" man in this excerpt from a letter to his first wife, Agnes Boulton O'Neill. It was written in 1920 from the bedside of his father, who had suffered a stroke and lay dying of intestinal cancer in a New York hospital.

TO AGNES BOULTON O'NEILL. ALS 4 pp. (Stationery headed: Lawrence and Memorial/Associated Hospitals/New London, Connecticut)

Thursday, p.m. / [July 29?, 1920]

Own Sweetheart: Am writing this at the hospital. Papa is lying in bed watching me, his strange eyes staring at me with a queer, uncanny wonder as if, in that veiled borderland between Life and Death in which his soul drifts suspended, a real living being of his own flesh and blood were an incongruous and puzzling spectacle. I feel as if my health, the sun tan on my face contrasted with the unearthly pallor of his, were a spiritual intrusion, an impudence. And yet how his eyes lighted up with grateful affection when he first saw me! It made me feel so glad, so happy I had come!

The situation is frightful! Papa is alive when he ought to be dead. The disease has eaten through his bowels. Internal decomposition has set in—while he is still living! There is a horrible, nauseating smell in the room, the sickening, overpowering odor of a dead thing. His face, his whole body is that of a corpse. He is unspeakably thin and wasted. Only his eyes are alive—and the light that glimmers through their glaze is remote and alien. He suffers incredible tortures—in spite of all their dope. Just a few moments ago he groaned in anguish and cried pitifully: "Oh God, why don't You take me! Why don't You take me!" And Mama and I silently echoed his prayer. But God seems to be in His Omnipotent mood just now and not in His All Merciful.

Travis Bogard and Jackson R. Bryer, eds., *Selected Letters of Eugene O'Neill.* New Haven, CT: Yale University Press, 1988, pp. 131–32.

Document 10: Thornton Wilder Fights for His Words

Thornton Wilder met Gertrude Stein, a well-known American writer and patron of the arts, when she gave a lecture in Chicago in 1934. Stein had been living for years in Paris with her partner, Alice B. Toklas. For more than a decade, Stein and Wilder were good friends as well as literary mentor and pupil, and their letters crisscrossed the Atlantic with comments on their works and words of encouragement. The following letter was written by Wilder in 1938, ten days before the opening of Our Town *in Princeton, New Jersey.*

To Gertrude Stein and Alice Toklas, Paris, France

12 January 1938   Century Club
think of it   7 West Forty-Third Street
                                                New York [New York]

Dear Ones:

Yes, faithless is what I am.

And even this spurt of fidelity is due to the fact that I have a sore throat and refuse to go to rehearsal and refuse to rewrite a certain scene in Act Two [of *Our Town*].

My only defense is that I have been faithless to everybody equally. I went to New Haven Christmas eve but by Christmas day at six o'clock I was back in New York *at work*. And similarly on New Year's day.

But that's not all.

Between work, there are fights.

As you predicted Jed [Harris, theatrical producer and director,] got the notion that he had written the play and was still writing it.

As long as his suggestions for alterations are on the structure they are often very good; but once they apply to the words they are always bad and sometimes atrocious.

There have been some white-hot flaring fights. At present we are in a lull of reconcilement.

The play opens a week from Saturday (Jan 22) in Princeton, New Jersey, for one night; then goes to Boston for two weeks; then enters New York.

Even with Jed's sentences in it—which I hope gradually to *abrade* away—it is a very good play. The cast is fine.

But that's not all:

Morning's—Jed's first phone calls don't start before noon, nor cease until 3 A.M.—mornings I'm hurriedly but joyously finishing up Play No #2 [*The Merchant of Yonkers*] for [Max] Reinhardt [theatrical producer and director] in California. . . .

Be patient with me a little longer. The hurly burly will soon be over.

You wouldn't know me and I don't know myself, but translated tho' I am I know that I love you more than tongue can tell.

Ever

Thy

Thornton

Edward Burns and Ulla E. Dyno, eds., with William Rice, *The Letters of Gertrude Stein and Thornton Wilder.* New Haven, CT: Yale University Press, 1996, pp. 205–207.

Document 11: Tennessee Williams's "Blue-Devils"

Some of Tennessee Williams's dramatic characters struggle with depression, alcoholism, and other problems and disorders with which Williams was all too familiar. Williams's sister, Rose, was given a prefrontal lobotomy for schizophrenia in 1938 and spent the rest of her life institutionalized. Williams battled addictions to alcohol and drugs and suffered from bouts of depression. In this 1943 letter to longtime friend and writer Donald Windham, Williams describes his troubled state of mind.

Metro-Goldwyn-Mayer Pictures, Culver City, Calif.

7/28/43

Dear Donnie:

I am glad another letter from you has come as I feel like writing you, it is so much better than talking to anyone else.

My nerves are tied in knots today. I have plunged into one of my periodic neuroses, I call them "blue-devils", and it is like having wild-cats under my skin. They are a Williams family trait, I suppose. Destroyed my sister's mind and made my father a raging drunkard. In me they take the form of interior storms that show remarkably little from the outside but which create a deep chasm between myself and all other people, even deeper than the relatively ordinary ones of homosexuality and being an artist. It is curious the various forms they take—someday, when I have the courage, I will sit down and face them and write them all out. Now I can only speak of the symptoms, for if I look at them too closely, I feel they would spring at me more violently. Now for instance all contact with people is like a salty finger stroking a raw wound. My office is merciful, but whenever the phone rings and someone raps at the door, I shudder and fairly cringe. Back of this craziness is a perfect sanity, untouched and wholly separate, a wise counsellor that looks for causes and tries to side-step effects and says patiently and comfortingly, Hang on, it will pass away! But knows that it will always return another day. Ever since I was about ten years old I have lived with these blue-devils of various kinds and degrees, they come and go, all of them at their crises achieving about the same intensity, none of them ever quite reaching the innermost me. All of us must sadly face the fact that we are make-shift arrangements.

It has done me good to write this out, I hope you don't mind. . . .

"The Gentleman Caller" remains my chief work, but it goes slowly, I feel no overwhelming interest in it. It lacks the violence that excites me, so I piddle around with it. My picture work is to make a scenario out of "Billy the Kid" material—as good an assignment I could hope for, but I am lazy about it and barely am started.

Love—

10.

P.S. Wrote this in depression which is now past and I am bright and sunny again.

Donald Windham, ed., *Tennessee Williams' Letters to Donald Windham 1940–1965*. New York: Holt, Rinehart, and Winston, 1976, pp. 91–94.

Document 12: Arthur Miller on the McCarthy Era

Beginning in 1947, Hollywood experienced some dark years as the House Un-American Activities Committee went on a witch hunt for Communists. The result was a blacklist that denied employment to those directors, producers, screenwriters, and actors named. Numerous playwrights were also caught in the quest. Arthur Miller was one of the playwright-screenwriters questioned by the committee. In an interview with Olga Carlisle and Rose Styron in 1966, he recalled how that episode in his life reminded him of stories about the Salem witch trials, on which his play The Crucible *is based.*

INTERVIEWER: What is the genesis of *The Crucible?*

MILLER: I thought of it first when I was at Michigan. I read a lot about the Salem witch trials at that time. Then when the McCarthy era came along, I remembered these stories and I used to tell them to people when it started. I had no idea that it was going to go as far as it went. I used to say, you know, [Senator Joseph] McCarthy is actually saying certain lines that I recall the witch-hunters saying in Salem. So I started to go back, not with the idea of writing a play, but to refresh my own mind because it was getting eerie. For example, his holding up his hand with cards in it, saying, "I have in my hand the names of so-and-so." Well, this was a standard tactic of seventeenth-century prosecutors confronting a witness who was reluctant or confused, or an audience in a church which was not quite convinced that this particular individual might be guilty. He wouldn't say, "I have in my hand a list . . . ," he'd say, "We possess the names of all these people who are guilty. But the time has not come yet to release them." He had nothing at all—he simply wanted to secure in the town's mind the idea that he saw everything, that everyone was transparent to him. It was a way of inflicting guilt on everybody, and many people responded genuinely out of guilt; some would come and tell him some fantasy, or something that they had done or thought that was evil in their minds.

Olga Carlisle and Rose Styron, "Arthur Miller," 1966, in *The Paris Review: Playwrights at Work*, ed. George Plimpton. New York: Modern Library, 2000, pp. 176–78.

Document 13: Lorraine Hansberry Disputes "Progress" in Racial Equality

In real life and in her dramas, Lorraine Hansberry spoke out against racial inequality. She wrote this letter to the New York

Times *in reference to civil disobedience and the Congress of Racial Equality's planned traffic "stall-in" (which failed) for the April 22 opening day of the 1964 World's Fair in Queens. In it, she tells of her own family's struggles in Chicago—the impetus behind her play* A Raisin in the Sun—*to explain the bitterness of the African American community.*

April 23, 1964

To the Editor,
The New York Times:

My father was typical of a generation of Negroes who believed that the "American way" could successfully be made to work to democratize the United States. Thus, twenty-five years ago, he spent a small personal fortune, his considerable talents, and many years of his life fighting, in association with NAACP attorneys, Chicago's "restrictive covenants" in one of this nation's ugliest ghettoes.

That fight also required that our family occupy the disputed property in a hellishly hostile "white neighborhood" in which, literally, howling mobs surrounded our house. One of their missiles almost took the life of the then eight-year-old signer of this letter. My memories of this "correct" way of fighting white supremacy in America include being spat at, cursed and pummeled in the daily trek to and from school. And I also remember my desperate and courageous mother, patrolling our house all night with a loaded German luger, doggedly guarding her four children, while my father fought the respectable part of the battle in the Washington court.

The fact that my father and the NAACP "won" a Supreme Court decision, in a now famous case which bears his name in the lawbooks, is—ironically—the sort of "progress" our satisfied friends allude to when they presume to deride the more radical means of struggle. The cost, in emotional turmoil, time and money, which led to my father's early death as a permanently embittered exile in a foreign country when he saw that after such sacrificial efforts the Negroes of Chicago were as ghetto-locked as ever, does not seem to figure in their calculations.

That is the reality that I am faced with when I now read that some Negroes my own age and younger say that we must now lie down in the streets, tie up traffic, do whatever we can—take to the hills with guns if necessary—and fight back. Fatuous people remark these days on our "bitterness." Why, of course we are bitter.

Sincerely,

Lorraine Hansberry

Lorraine Hansberry, *To Be Young, Gifted, and Black: Lorraine Hansberry in Her Own Words*, adapted by Robert Nemiroff. Englewood Cliffs, NJ: Prentice-Hall, 1969, pp. 20–21.

For Further Research

Joseph Quincy Adams, *A Life of William Shakespeare*. Boston: Houghton Mifflin, 1925.

William Archer, ed. and trans., *The Collected Works of Henrik Ibsen*, vols. 1–7. New York: Charles Scribner's Sons, 1906.

Barron's Simply Shakespeare: Romeo and Juliet. New York: Barron's Education Series, 2002.

Ben Jonson's Plays, vols. 1–2. Introduction by Felix E. Schelling. London: J.M. Dent & Sons, 1964.

Eric Bentley, *The Life of the Drama*. New York: Atheneum, 1964.

Christopher Bigsby, ed., *The Portable Arthur Miller*. New York: Penguin Books, 1995.

Biography.com, A&E Television Networks, www.biography.com.

Aurobindo Bose, trans., *Later Poems of Rabindranath Tagore*. London: Peter Owen, 1974.

Pratima Bowes, trans., *Some Songs and Poems from Rabindranath Tagore*. London: East West, 1984.

Roger Boxill, *Tennessee Williams*. London: Macmillan, 1987.

Enoch Brater, *Why Beckett*. London: Thames and Hudson, 1989.

Steven R. Carter, *Hansberry's Drama: Commitment Amid Complexity*. Urbana and Chicago: University of Illinois Press, 1991.

Richard Ellmann, *Four Dubliners*. New York: George Braziller, 1987.

Angel Flores, ed., *Ibsen*. Trans. Jenny Covan. New York: Haskell House, 1966.

John Gassner, *Masters of the Drama*. New York: Dover, 1940.

Leon Golden, trans., *Aristotle's Poetics: A Translation and Commentary for Students of Literature*. Commentary by O.B. Hardison. Englewood, NJ: Prentice-Hall, 1968.

Thomas Blenman Hare, *Zeami's Style: The Noh Plays of Zeami Motokiyo*. Stanford, CA: Stanford University Press, 1986.

Rupert Hart-Davis, ed., *The Letters of Oscar Wilde*, by Oscar Wilde. New York: Harcourt, Brace & World, 1962.

Anthony Holden, *William Shakespeare: The Man Behind the Genius*. Boston: Little, Brown, 1999.

Louis Kronenberger, *Oscar Wilde*. Boston: Little, Brown, 1976.

Petri Liukkonen, "Author's Calendar," Pegasos, www.kirjasto.sci.fi/calendar.htm.

Hugh Lloyd-Jones, trans., *The Eumenides*, by Aeschylus. Englewood Cliffs, NJ: Prentice-Hall, 1970.

Brian Masters, *A Student's Guide to Molière*. London: Heinemann Educational Books, 1970.

Siegried Melchinger, *Anton Chekhov*. Trans. Edith Tarcov. New York: Frederick Ungar, 1972.

Michael Meyer, trans., *Henrik Ibsen—Plays: Two*. London: Methuen Drama, 1965.

Carl R. Mueller and Anna Krajewska-Wieczorek, trans., *Sophokles: The Complete Plays*. Hanover, NH: Smith and Kraus, 2000.

Charles Nicholl, *The Reckoning: The Murder of Christopher Marlowe*. New York: Harcourt Brace, 1992.

Garry O'Connor, *William Shakespeare: A Life*. London: Hodder & Stoughton, 1991.

John Oxenford, trans., *Autobiography of Johann Wolfgang von Goethe*, by Goethe. New York: Horizon Press, 1969.

John Pilling, *Samuel Beckett*. London: Routledge & Kegan Paul, 1976.

Christopher Ricks, ed., *The New History of Literature*. Vol. 3, *English Drama to 1710*. New York: Peter Bedrick Books, 1987.

J. Thomas Rimer and Yamazaki Masakazu, trans., *On the Art of the Nō Drama: The Major Treatises of Zeami*, by Zeami. Princeton, NJ: Princeton University Press, 1984.

Carl Rollyson, ed., *Critical Survey of Drama*. 2nd rev. ed. Pasadena, CA: Salem Press, 2003.

Erich Segal, ed., *Euripides: A Collection of Critical Essays*. Englewood Cliffs, NJ: Prentice-Hall, 1968.

Louis Sheaffer, *O'Neill: Son and Playwright*. Boston: Little, Brown, 1968.

C.P. Sinha, *Eugene O'Neill's Tragic Vision*. New Delhi: New Statesman, 1981.

David R. Slavitt and Palmer Bovie, eds., *Euripides*. Vols. 1–4. Philadelphia: University of Pennsylvania Press, 1997.

Hermann Stresau, *Thornton Wilder*. Trans. Frieda Schutze. New York: Frederick Ungar, 1971.

Josiah Symon, *Shakespeare the Englishman*. New York: Haskell House, 1971.

TheatreHistory.com, www.theatrehistory.com.

John Whaley, trans., *Goethe: Selected Poems*. Evanston, IL: Northwestern University Press, 1998.

Tennessee Williams, *Tennessee Williams Memoirs*. Garden City, NY: Doubleday, 1911.

Index